The Return of the Chaos Monsters —
and Other Backstories of the Bible

The Return of the Chaos Monsters —
and Other Backstories of the Bible

Gregory Mobley

WILLIAM B. EERDMANS PUBLISHING COMPANY
GRAND RAPIDS, MICHIGAN / CAMBRIDGE, U.K.

Published 2012 by
Wm. B. Eerdmans Publishing Co.
2140 Oak Industrial Drive N.E., Grand Rapids, Michigan 49505 /
P.O. Box 163, Cambridge CB3 9PU U.K.

Printed in the United States of America

17 16 15 14 13 12   7 6 5 4 3 2 1

Library of Congress Cataloging-in-Publication Data

Mobley, Gregory, 1957-
The return of the chaos monsters — and other backstories of the Bible /
Gregory Mobley.
p.   cm.
ISBN 978-0-8028-3746-2 (pbk.: alk. paper)
1. Bible. O.T. — Criticism, Narrative.   I. Title.

BS1182.3.M63   2012
221.6′6 — dc23

2011026645

www.eerdmans.com

To Carole Ann McDaniel Mobley

Contents

Contents

Acknowledgments

I am grateful to so many: to Tom Raabe and Allen Myers at Eerdmans; to Mark Burrows, Matthew Myer Boulton, T. J. Wray, and Mark Heim of Andover Newton; to Arthur Green, Judith Kates, Jonah Steinberg, and Or Rose of Hebrew College; to friends Don and Theresa Sull, Joseph Bassett, and Steve Schmidt.

I am indebted to many bright students at Harvard Divinity School, Union Theological, Andover Newton, and Hebrew College who first heard — and often first articulated — these ideas in classes on the Bible.

I am grateful to my daughter Esther for her keen editorial eye and intellectual companionship. Gregory and Tommy: I hope you hear me speaking to you in these pages. Oh, Dad, I love and admire you so much, and you more than anyone else know why I can only dedicate this book to Mom.

But I cannot merely thank the people of whose benefits I am conscious. I must also thank a host of benefactors I never knew or have forgotten whose survival skills, kindness, and faithfulness to duty granted me safe conduct to this day. As I pause here to express gratitude, I stand in awe before a mystery as great as those forty weeks I spent in the wilderness of unconsciousness. I am not clueless; I have diaries, memory bytes, my own testimony, and the countertestimony of many companions on this immense journey, but a lot of important things happened before I started keeping records. Before my literacy, before my orality, even before my nativity. I will never solve the true mystery. Finally, then, I can only thank God.

56,481.

That is how many words are in my manuscript.

And they were not enough, and adding more would not get me any closer to the goal I failed to reach.

I never found the words to say what I wanted to express about the Bible, but I cannot resist a final attempt. If this works, and I pray it does not, readers need not read another word.

In this book I wanted to say something about the entire Bible from Genesis to Revelation, from Dan to Beersheba, and so I climbed to the highest place I could find. East of Edenic Canaan, I ascended Mount Nebo to stand on the rock where Moses stood. I looked over Jordan and what did I see?

I saw Abraham and Sarah, and Moses, and Samson and Delilah, and Rizpah, and Jesus, and Mary and Martha, and Paul and Silas. I kept looking and I saw Hillel and Shammai, and Origen and Tertullian. In the landscape of the Bible, millions more appeared to me: Jews and Gentiles, Crusaders and Saracens, Celts who stayed on the mainland and Celts who sailed to the British Isles, African Americans and Scots-Irish Americans and Cherokees, Yankees and Confederates and those who were neither, the peoples of the Border States. In the pages of the Bible I saw everyone I have ever known, my family, my friends, my rivals.

I looked into the Bible and, lo and behold, I could swear I saw the whole wide world in its hands, in and between its lines.

The Seven Backstories

1. **God has subdued chaos, just barely.**
   CHAPTER ONE
   The Return of the Chaos Monsters:
   The Backstory of Creation

2. **God has given humans an instruction manual for life on planet Earth so they can partner with God in the management of chaos.**
   CHAPTER TWO
   It's Love That Makes the World Go 'Round:
   The Backstory of Torah

3. **God has enacted the tough love of moral cause and effect in order to reward fidelity to the instruction manual and to support management of the chaos.**
   CHAPTER THREE
   Poetic Justice:
   The Backstory of the Former Prophets

4. **God enlists prophets to mediate this dynamic partnership upon which the health of creation depends.**
   CHAPTER FOUR
   Anger Management:
   The Backstory of the Latter Prophets

5. **Through praise humans release energy that augments God's management of chaos; through lament humans report on the quality of God's management of chaos.**
   CHAPTER FIVE
   God Needs Us:
   The Backstory of the Psalms

6. **Here and there, humans catch glimpses of the divine design for chaos management; living according to these insights is another expression of the partnership.**
   CHAPTER SIX
   The Blueprint:
   The Backstory of Wisdom

7. **There are times when chaos gains the upper hand and humans in partnership with God can only hope that God is able, as in the beginning, to subdue chaos.**
   CHAPTER SEVEN
   Conspiracy Theory:
   The Backstory of Apocalyptic

Backstories

---

1. God has subdued chaos, just barely.

2. God has given humans an instruction manual for life on planet Earth so they can partner with God in the management of chaos.

3. God has enacted the tough love of moral cause and effect in order to reward fidelity to the instruction manual and to support management of the chaos.

4. God enlists prophets to mediate this dynamic partnership upon which the health of creation depends.

5. Through praise humans release energy that augments God's management of chaos; through lament humans report on the quality of God's management of chaos.

6. Here and there, humans catch glimpses of the divine design for chaos management; living according to these insights is another expression of the partnership.

7. There are times when chaos gains the upper hand and humans in partnership with God can only hope that God is able, as in the beginning, to subdue chaos.

That is one way to tell the story of the Bible.

This book is about the stories in the Bible and the stories behind the Bible and how the Bible is essentially, relentlessly story. This book is about seven basic stories — outlined above — that the book known to Jews as

Tanakh[1] and to Christians as the Old Testament tells as its composers and the ancient communities to whom they spoke wrestled with a single theme: how to make meaning from the chaos of experience, the human condition.

As we — my gentle readers and yours truly — begin this journey through the stories of the Bible, allow me this word about my intentions and inclinations. I am passionate about the Bible. I am *passionate,* and that can be a problem. There are times when my feelings totally overpower my thoughts. I am passionate about the *Bible,* and that can be a problem too. There are times when I lose any perspective about all other holy books and all their brilliant interpreters and I cannot believe anyone would waste time on them when we have the Bible.

I am passionate about stories, and about the way that humans tell stories to themselves and each other in order to make sense of the chaos. There are stories that humans have been telling ever since they wandered off the savannas of the southern trough of the Great Rift Valley. There is something incredible about the Bible and those stories. About 3,500 years ago, the ancient Lebanese invented the alphabet, and within 500 years of that, this new technology had spread to Greece and Israel, cultures located on and next to the northern trough of the Great Rift Valley. And so we have from the dawn of literacy two big text witnesses, Homer and Bible, at this turning point, this axial age when the old world of orality gave way to the new world of literacy. Homer and Bible represent two huge arks built just as the flood of alphabetic writing began to inundate the thousand and one stories of that preliterate world whose lifespan makes our mere three millennia of alphabetic literacy seem but as yesterday when it is past and like a watch in the night.

Onto the ark of Bible they came two by two: all the stories and characters of the old oral world. Adam and Eve, and all the mythic wisdom and confusion about what it means to be gendered. Cain and Abel, the farmer and the cowman, and the perennial struggle between competing economies. Isaac and Ishmael, the smooth man and the hairy man, city mouse and country mouse. Samson and Delilah, representing impulse and cunning, their relationship an emblem of how vulnerable love makes us. Elder brother and younger brother, and how some of us end up alienated in a far country and some just as alienated when we never leave the farm but allow resentments to bar us from entering the father's house.

Every time I walk through the ark of Bible, I notice more of these pri-

---

1. Tanakh is an acronym for the Jewish Bible built from its three sections: Torah, Nevi'im, and Ketuvim, i.e., Instruction, Prophets, and Writings.

meval pairs lurking in the holds and wandering around on deck: serpents and rainbows, heroes who complete their odysseys home from war and heroes who do not, male heroes who get trapped in an underworld and the female heroes who rescue them, and the actors in all those role-reversal scenarios involving first and last, older and younger, Dives and Lazarus. Up the gangplank they come, the dragon of chaos, the natural man, the seven antediluvian sages who gave gifts of culture to humans, the seven heroes, the four demons. They bring with them their stories of the flood, of the plague, of the quest, of combats and courtships, of Edens and Armageddons. The biblical writers shaped these characters and plots to fit into the peculiar shape of their ark, with its kosher fare, Hebrew idioms, and, above all, its enigmatic, elusive Almighty, YHWH.

I love how the ark of Bible has borne variations of these stories, the treasures of darkness, the wisdom and humanity of the old oral world, into the brave new world of literacy, and now, the braver new world of digital communication. Accidentally or providentially, the Bible contains a share of the oral traditions of aeons. This omnibus volume of everything — laws, rites, legends — wrangled into rough shape, into a single narrative by a succession of Judahite redactors, is one of our first witnesses to alphabetic literacy. As such, it records the lore of the preliterate generations. The Bible does not have every story ever told, but it has many. This is why the Bible echoes with archetypes. Its parallels to the literature of other cultures are not Jungian; they are Dickensian.

So much has changed and is changing before our eyes as humans experience the conflicts, confusion, and creativity of a new pivot, a new turning, a new axial age through the World Wide Web. And yet for all that change, I am still moved and absolutely understand why Adam and Eve felt ashamed and wanted to hide from the Lord God after eating of the tree of knowledge, and why Moses felt so alone as he tried to balance a vision of the living God with the reality of a complaining congregation, and why David cried when he heard that Absalom, his son and enemy, was dead, and why Mary sang when the Holy Spirit stirred new life inside her, even if that song was both hymn and lament, sorrow and love mingled down.

There it is, even if I cannot quite capture it in words. I invite readers to join me as we search together, across millennia, continents, cultures, and media, for deep things, for ultimate concerns, for those truths that were at the beginning, are now, and ever shall be, about what it means to be human in a world that was created. This is the tale that the seven backstories of the Bible narrate.

The Bible and Story

The storylike nature of Scripture extends beyond the narratives everyone knows about Adam and Eve in the garden and the paired animals in Noah's ark or the proverbs we hear every day about the patience of Job and the charity of the Good Samaritan. Even the dreary parts of Holy Writ — the genealogies of Genesis, the lists in Leviticus — are framed as part of a story, neither appendices in the back of the book nor footnotes at the bottom of the page. Even the "begats" function as links in the chain of cause and effect through their insertion into primeval and patriarchal sagas. Even the legalese appears as words that Moses spoke from Mount Sinai. Everything has a setting in a story.

Liturgical poetry becomes story through prefixed introductions that associate given psalms with events in the life of David. In the books of Proverbs and Ecclesiastes, the ascription of proverbial couplets and philosophical paragraphs to Solomon imparts a background and characterization that invite readers to imagine and identify with their world-weary composer in a way that disembodied "quotes of the day" or abstract meditations on the human condition cannot. Collections of prophetic speeches are prefaced with profiles of the seers whose jeremiads follow and the bumbling monarchs they harassed ("The word of the LORD that came to Hosea . . . in the days of Kings Uzziah, Jotham, Ahaz, and Hezekiah," Hos. 1:1 NRSV).[2] Much of the Bible is story, and even those parts that did not begin that way have evolved into stories as they have been edited and interpreted. When Judahite priests in the sixth century B.C.E. Babylonian exile wanted to preserve as much memory as possible of the Jerusalem temple, not for *auld lang syne* but so it could be rebuilt, they did not draw up blueprints. They inscribed their memories in stories about the wilderness tent from Exodus, and Solomon's temple from 1 Kings.

These dreary parts of Torah — lists of territorial boundaries and of clan ancestors and of temple measurements — did not begin as stories. The biblical composers of Exodus, Leviticus, and Numbers, for example, likely bundled together legal codes from many sources and eras and then secondarily placed them in the mouth and time of Moses. The psalms acquired Davidic backstories after their original composition. A narrative alchemy is at work in the process of the Bible that endlessly, inevitably seeks to transform every genre into story. Those parts of the Bible that were

---

2. Unless otherwise indicated, the biblical quotations in this book are my translation.

most resistant to this process had delayed conversions. The book of Lamentations, for example, existed in a narrative vacuum in its earliest canonical location among the miscellany of the Writings in the Jewish Bible. In the sequence of the Christian Bible, however, its placement next to the book and association with the person of Jeremiah ensured that it would be read in conjunction with the sixth century B.C.E. destruction of Jerusalem by the Babylonians; it is now part of that story. In rabbinic Judaism, the practice of reading Lamentations on a certain Jewish holiday, the ninth of Ab, a day of lamentation for more than one temple, did the same. The New Testament epistles remain hard to corral within the boundary of narrative, but that has not deterred generations of wranglers from attempting to pull them with cords of commentary into a reconstructed story of the early church.

We are so accustomed to the narrative fabric of the Bible that we may not appreciate that there are other ways to compose an omnibus volume of a culture's religious teachings, that is, a bible. The Qur'an is a series of speeches; the Talmud a series of conversations. The religious geniuses who created the Torah in the middle of the first millennium B.C.E., the world's first Bible known as the Pentateuch, cast it as a story, and that determined the genre for the Jewish and Christian revisions of Torah that followed. The Jewish Bible grew to include the Prophets (Nevi'im) and Writings (Ketuvim); the Christian Bible added the New Testament to the Tanakh that had resulted from the former achievement. The Talmud and Qur'an contain stories, but neither is essentially or finally story.

It is as if there is a software program that the transgenerational community of biblical composers, editors, and interpreters share that makes meaning through story. What is it about stories that make them such a powerful vehicle for bearing religious meaning through time?

What Is a Story?

The poet and literary critic Jane Hirshfield wrote, "Narrative . . . uses the structure of time to defeat the ephemerality of time."[3] "The ephemerality of time" refers to the fact that time marches on, time flies, and time waits for no one. The moment does not even allow for clarity or insight. What

---

3. Jane Hirshfield, *Nine Gates: Entering the Mind of Poetry* (New York: HarperCollins, 1998), 183.

really did happen? What was the story? Narratives create chains of events bound by cause and effect along a timeline, allowing us to pin down a story before it slips away. Once the story is told, the chaos of experience assumes shape, direction, motive, and episodes. *This led to that which led to this which led to that.*

In the fast-forward of events, stories allow us to imagine that we are able to hit the pause button of reality and record and rewind, even though we cannot. Narrative allows for us to compose an account of what happened, even if what the narrative said happened, never happened. Once we have a story, we have direction, shape, motive, and episodes. We no longer have chaos; we have meaning and order. And the story we create will represent this meaning and order. Since there is no rewind button, the story is all we have to represent the order we have created until we author or adopt a new story. Genesis 1 is correct: the ordered world was and is created through the agency of divine language; John 1 too: in the beginning was the Word, the *logos,* the story.

Humans are storytellers, meaning-makers, and pattern-tracers. Even before we learn to count, we are constantly putting two and two together, tying episodes together into the daisy-chain cause-and-effect sequences we know as stories. We hear songs on the radio and pull them into the soundtrack of our lives by associating them with struggles and scenes from our adventures. We watch films and overwrite the screenplays with our own: we see ourselves in the hero; that family is just like my childhood neighbors; that actress or actor is my old girlfriend or boyfriend. Man does not live by bread alone, but by stories. And each story leads to another as our minds seek to interpret, connect, and harmonize each new story into that single masterpiece we all author, consciousness's *magnum opus,* every soul's work, the Song of Myself.

We are caught in narrative's web. A few humans actually pen autobiographies, but every sentient soul participates in the privacy of that form of internal storytelling we know as consciousness. Believers imagine that a divine Listener hears this latter story. The task of theology is the linking of our individual story to the biggest story we can imagine. The most esoteric realms of religious thought, such as Jewish mystical Kabbalah, dare to explore the divine consciousness, reading all of Torah as the autobiography of God.

And at the end of each day, after we arrive home from our adventures, we pull off an architectural miracle. Every lonely mortal graced with companionship spins the subsequent chapter of a serial novel. We construct ornate cathedrals of narrative out of the odd materials we picked up along the way, mortared by our own linguistic version of the same bitumen and pitch that the Hebrew biblical writers had in their workshops of syntax, the narrative *vav*, a special form of the Hebrew "and." "So I got to work late *and then* my boss told me X, *and then* I told her Y, *and then, and then, and then*." The composers of biblical prose appended the simplest conjunction, "and," to a line, gave it a little extra vocalization (it is pronounced *vah* — not *veh* — when it performs this binding function), doubled the initial consonant of the word to which the "and" was attached, and *voila*: the Biblical Hebrew "and then."[4] "There was light *and then* God saw that the light was good *and then* there was evening *and then* there was morning, *and then and then and then*," before you know it, you are standing with Moses on Mount Nebo at the end of Deuteronomy, light-years from when God first peered over the abyss. We are so adept at this meaning-making through narrative that we can do it in our sleep, a dozen times every night, often with bizarre results. This book celebrates biblical storytelling and emphasizes the ways that the Bible makes meaning through narrative.

Backstories and Metanarratives

The Bible is "not always as deep as we think."[5] That is what Krister Stendahl, biblical scholar, bishop, theologian, and ecumenicist, this prince of Christendom, wrote in one of the last essays he penned. To say that the Bible is "not as deep as we think" is not to say it is shallow. It is to say that the Bible contains a basic repertoire of stories and teachings that are easily apprehended. This book argues that the entire span of the Hebrew Bible, known in Judaism as Tanakh and in Christianity as the Old Testament, tells seven basic stories and that these primary narratives are connected to the larger pool of stories that humans have been telling ever since we first wandered off the savannas of the southern Rift Valley. The title of the most popular story on planet Earth is and always has been "What I Did Today," and despite its infinite tellings, twists, and turns, it always ends with the same refrain, "and I made it home."

4. This element of Hebrew syntax is known to generations of students as the *waw consecutive*.

5. Krister Stendahl, "Why I Love the Bible," in *Meanings: The Bible as Document and Guide*, 2nd ed. (Minneapolis: Fortress, 2008), 249.

All the near misses, all the daring feats of food acquisition and companion acquisition (i.e., all adventures and romances, respectively), all the intrigues with corrupt officials, high sheriffs, and cunning clerics, all the combats with monsters and masked outlaws, all the couplings and seductions — all these epic particulars are memorable inflations of the quotidian. The Bible, mostly composed in ancient Jerusalem on a geologic shelf overlooking the northern Rift Valley, is deep — what could be deeper than these enduring stories about what it means to be human in a world that was created? — but divines, scholars, and armchair civilian cipherists have overread and obscured its elegant simplicity in order to create lodge secrets for their respective subcultures of readers.

A student who had spent time in Hollywood once remarked during a class discussion of folklore motifs that screenwriters have a truism that there are only six — or seven or eight or ten — basic stories. This adage with its numerical imprecision is, I suspect, proverbial, but if there is such a list, it surely includes the following:

1. "Fish out of Water" in all its rural/urban, high-class/low-class, masquerading variations (the theme of most comedies).
2. "What Goes Up Must Come Down," as a titan falls from Olympian heights and becomes a human being in the process (the theme of most dramas; or "comedies" in the Classical sense; i.e., these stories end on an uptick, with the Harlequin smiling).
3. "Whatsoever a Man Soweth That Shall He Also Reap" (the theme of most detective or crime narratives and tragedies).[6]

We could all draw up our own lists. In the 1950s, horror and science fiction genre films and comic books were filled with benign insects and reptiles that morphed into gargantuan monsters after they had been inadvertently injected with some steroid of nuclear fallout. Recent movies traffic in a different type of monster, zombie vampires: lost souls, physically primed and sexually charged, who exist to cannibalize poor victims minding their own business. Cold War anxieties about nuclear war have mutated into postmodern fears about mindless, soulless consumers who feed on each other socially and sexually. Do we have a new story, "The Rise of the Zombie Vampires"? As it turns out, zombie vampires are old news and

---

6. Judith Skelton Grant, ed., *For Your Eyes Only: The Letters of Robertson Davies* (New York: Viking, 1999), 109.

their story is as old as the hills, or at least as old as the Bible. It is the topic of the first chapter of this book, "The Return of the Chaos Monsters," the backstory of biblical creation stories, not to mention virtually every contemporary horror story or film.

The premise of this book is that the Bible is best understood as wholly narrative, and that most of its individual narratives are variations on seven basic stories, and that all seven of these stories are variations on a single theme: the dynamic interplay of order and chaos. This basic corpus of foundational narratives, the seven backstories of our title, undergirds each respective section of the Bible.

Some but not all of these basic narratives in Scripture can be labeled "backstories." A backstory is an implied or yet-to-be-composed narrative that is the necessary prologue to an existing story. Backstories are the prequels to the stories we hear, read, and narrate. *Star Wars* episodes I-III function as the backstory to the original film of 1977. J. R. R. Tolkien's *The Hobbit* is the backstory to the *Lord of the Rings* trilogy. Of making many backstories there is no end because no story starts "in the beginning." Every infant story is born into a narrative world that already exists. Every story begins in the middle of things. Even though the Bible claims to start "in the beginning," observant readers of the first two verses of Genesis note that even there, at daybreak on creation morning, we are already midstream. There is something there: the primeval cosmic soup with its formless abyss, the face of the waters over which the divine wind hovers.

Narrative art is not just arithmetic, but mathematics: it has negative numbers so that the zero starting point of any tale is no barrier to further computations. The *Star Wars* films with the lowest numbered episodes and Tolkien's *Hobbit* function as backstories, though they now stand on their own as narratives with their own legitimacy and standing. They no longer possess the mystery of a true implied narrative or backstory. The latter has not yet been composed, but looms, all latency, just before the horizon of a given narrative's daybreak. A backstory is the prequel not yet in production, the matrix for which every orphan story searches, Narrative's Eve.

For example, the subject of chapter 1 of this book, "The Return of the Chaos Monsters," is the backstory for biblical creation narratives. Sometimes creation narratives in the Bible clearly assume this backstory, as when the prophet Isaiah talks about how the Lord will slay the dragon of chaos, Leviathan, on the last day (Isa. 27:1), or when Job requests the services of a flautist capable of charming the primeval serpent from its basket, so that all hell might break loose and the calendar rewind from the worst week of his life all the way back to the formless void and deep darkness of the midnight before creation morning (Job 3:8). On other occasions, the biblical composers of creation narratives depend on their audiences' knowledge of this backstory about the monsters even as they defy the conventional pattern and change the plot. The drama beneath the surface of Genesis 1:21 ("*and then* God created the great dragons") is its casual dismissal of the importance of the chaos monsters. In Genesis 1, they are not God's mythological opponents; they are merely one more phylum of creation alongside the fish and fowl with whom they share day five and whose features they grotesquely combine.

Others of these basic stories in Scripture can be termed "metanarratives." A *meta*narrative (*meta* is Greek for "beyond") is an articulation of the global story that a series of local stories or discrete episodes tell and retell with different details, settings, and characters. So, for example, the subject of chapter 3, "Poetic Justice," is the big story beyond, behind, or above the scores of little stories that make up the Former Prophets, the biblical books of Joshua, Judges, Samuel, and Kings. New backdrops and characters are hurriedly ushered on stage just as soon as the previous scenes end. Joshua and Rahab give way to Samson and Delilah, then to David and Bathsheba, then to Elijah and Jezebel, but the theme is always the same: there is a symmetrical design to divine justice, and whatsoever a man soweth, that (precisely, tit for tat, measure for measure) shall he reap.

*Back*stories, *meta*narratives: whatever prepositional prefix we choose, these terms indicate that there is no single dry bone of a story. Single stories combine through sinews of shared backgrounds and understandings to create bodies of stories — words made flesh — that depend on, mutually inform, and beget each other. *Dem bones, dem stories;* the ankle bone is connected to the shin bone, and so are the stories we hear and narrate connected to implied and potential stories behind and beyond them.

Deep Story

There are ways of looking at stories that inspect them not from above, surveying their contents, but from the side, in cross section, surveying their form. Loosely described as forms of "structuralism," they change the orientation of the reader so that it is possible to see themes that lie beneath the surface of a narrative. One such method was developed by the

Russian folklorist Vladimir Propp, who wrote about recurring patterns in fairy tales.[7]

Propp observed that the many Russian fairy tales he analyzed about Ivans, Baba Yagas, wild geese, and czarinas contained a limited number of distinct movements: a family member, for instance, goes missing; a sibling sets out on the search; the hero encounters donors and dangers, receives tokens and tools, and embarks on the quest that ends back home with the family reunited, a marriage, or some happily-ever-after resolution. Propp constructed an abstract presentation of these movements, a table that delineates the full inventory of possible events in a tale. No single fairy tale contains all the variations, but, Propp insisted, the sequence of these "functions," his term for these distinct developments, is fixed. The wayward siblings must get lost before they get found. The hero has to acquire the token that seems trivial but proves indispensable — like Jack's bean that grows into the stalk — before venturing into the zone of adventure. The monster has to be defeated before the wedding of the hero.[8]

There is something in Propp's scheme about the course of life: elders use the fairy tales to sketch the map of what lies around the next developmental bend and to program their juniors above all else to be resourceful, able to transform every odd encounter, trivial experience, and random acquisition into the donors, ordeals, and magical tools necessary to complete their adventure. The fairy tales prepare children for life by previewing its stages: leaving home, gaining proficiencies and craft through struggle, and making a new home with a companion. The fairy tales dispense self-confidence through the traditional wisdom that the child already possesses all the skills necessary to make it without the parent if he or she will creatively adapt or draw on his or her own inventory of abilities and experiences. The strangely colored pebble that oddly attracted your attention before you put it in your pocket will be the missile that blinds the ogre; the stray dog that you fed and who now follows you will bark to alert you to the approach of a nocturnal attacker.

Such narratives about quests and heroes were the premodern precur-

---

7. Vladimir Propp, *The Morphology of the Folktale*, trans. L. Scott, 2nd ed. (Austin: University of Texas Press, 1960).

8. Though it is merely a rhetorical ploy to disarm his readers, W. Somerset Maugham's opening sentences of his novel *The Razor's Edge* (1944) capture the often unconscious expectations we share for the structure of "proper" stories: "I have never begun a novel with more misgiving. If I call it a novel it is only because I don't know what else to call it. I have little story to tell and I end neither with a death nor a marriage."

sors to developmental psychology, only rather than producing charts of the stages of life in the style of Erik Erikson, ancient storytellers encoded this information into stories. The actual adventure in the tale is not about its presenting details, but about something deeper, something below the surface, namely, growing up.[9] The surface details are, however, important. The larger-than-life characters, outlandish scenarios, and talking animals are the special effects that make the tale entertaining enough to be heard and memorable enough to be passed on.

A scholar of classical Greek literature and religion, Walter Burkert, has used Propp's tools to dig even deeper into the meaning of tales about the quest.[10] Burkert notes a striking correspondence between the sequences of events in fairy tales and the biological imperatives that propel human behavior.[11] Burkert's thesis in *Creation of the Sacred* (1996) — and he finds evidence for it in studies of rats searching for food in university mazes and primates learning sign language in Atlanta laboratories — is that the basic structure of the Proppian tale narrates the story of food acquisition. The hero leaves home, forages and fights, and returns home with the means for family survival. So, as it turns out, we live to tell our tales. The tale is about the fact that we survived the adventure. For this reason, listeners must always beware: just as the winners write the history, it is the survivors who narrate the tale. For this reason, we can understand the deep appeal of sad stories. The fact that there is someone alive to narrate the tragedy is its own kind of triumph. In their very telling, even the stories about loss affirm survival.

So the tale is about the adventure it narrates. It is also, at a deeper level, about growing up. Deeper still, the tale that begins with a quest and ends with a marriage is about biological survival, about the acquisition of food and a partner for reproduction.

These observations about deep meanings below the surface of stories are not meant to reduce the transporting music of stories with their rich array of details, locales, and characters to an inert list of functions and abstractions. Structural analysis, if pressed too far, becomes the know-it-all Freudian conversation stopper, "It's all about sex." The tale is and yet is not

9. As demonstrated for the Babylonian Gilgamesh epic by Thorkild Jacobsen in *The Treasures of Darkness: A History of Mesopotamian Religion* (New Haven: Yale University Press, 1976), 219.

10. Walter Burkert, *Creation of the Sacred: Tracks of Biology in Early Religions* (Cambridge: Harvard University Press, 1996).

11. Burkert, *Creation of the Sacred*, 56-67.

merely about sex or food or power. We should not pit the beautiful landscape of the surface details and social, psychological, and biological deep functions against each other.

Rather, we should think of the relation between content and form in stories as analogous to the interaction of melody and rhythm in music. Much of the reason why music *moves* us is rhythmic. Pulsation and respiration link up with the rhythm of the music in ways that lead us, depending on the genre and our own sensibilities, to tremble, tremble, tremble, or sway, or rock, or roll; to tap our feet, to internally join heartbeat to backbeat. Rhythm produces this satisfying physiological response. But you still need a tune to hum. The melody provides the mental colors and details that capture imaginations and trigger emotions at the same time that the rhythm ensures that the music penetrates deeper and gets into our bones. The in-and-outs of the Proppian functions, the sequence of episodes, in all their beguiling and apparent novelty, divert us and entertain us so that we sit still long enough to absorb the message, never realizing that this is a tune we have heard many times before.

The Seven Backstories

The backstories and metanarratives observed in subsequent chapters are not primarily about the sociobiological subterranean strata of the literature in the Bible. Yet they are about themes that are deeper than the presenting details in any single biblical text. They are about the meaning-making most characteristic of each respective genre of the Hebrew Bible, understood here as (1) the creation stories, (2) the Pentateuchal narratives and teachings, (3) the didactic stories in the Former Prophets, (4) the oracles in the Latter Prophets, (5) the liturgical poetry of the Psalter, (6) the maxims and essays in the Wisdom literature, and (7) the visions and scenarios of apocalyptic. Seven genres; seven backstories. In the end, the elucidation of these seven backstories provides a thematic overview of the entire Hebrew Bible.

Theologians use the term "theodicy" to describe attempts to understand ultimate justice. Why do bad things happen to good people? How can God be all-powerful and wholly good, given the enormity of cosmic suffering? There is a sense in which all our storytelling, meaning-making, and pattern-tracing are works of theodicy. Whether we find injustice or justice, we search for connections, supply motives, and construct stories in order to make sense of each aspect of the face of reality we glimpse. We imagine meaning in the facial gestures of others; we assign blame for every failure and discover a hero for every success; we obsessively compete with each other to provide a more satisfying account of what just happened and why. We are constantly processing, editing, and revising the story in our minds. Similarly, each genre of biblical literature has its own governing metanarrative or subservient backstory that informs the way it performs the function of theodicy, making sense by building arks of narrative that preserve meaning and create order amidst the flood of incidents and accidents that threatens to sweep us away in its currents. The backstory of each genre of biblical literature offers its own theodicy, its own style of wrestling with the chaos that threatens to make existence meaningless.

1. The backstory of the creation stories is the Return of the Chaos Monsters, humanity's all-time favorite B movie. The chaos monsters are personifications of the disorderly, random, and untamed features of reality. This backstory explains that God has defeated but not obliterated the monsters, and that they invariably return to wreak havoc when humans inadvertently open the door to their cages through ethical lapses.

2. The backstory of the legal sections of the Pentateuch, the Mosaic law, is It's Love That Makes the World Go 'Round, that is, that human virtue buttresses God's great work of cosmic management. This backstory is the necessary complement to the return of the chaos monsters. The Mosaic Torah is, in the biblical view, nothing less than the instruction manual for life on planet Earth. The persons and communities who live according to its patterns and progressions help God maintain the fragile triumph of order over chaos.

3. The narratives of Joshua-Judges-Samuel-Kings, the Former Prophets, work out, one story at a time, the implications of the Mosaic instruction, demonstrating how God governs human fortunes according to moral cause and effect. These stories do not leave much room for chaos — their physics is Newtonian, not quantum — and the Bible will later present a counternarrative (the story of Job) to these moralistic fables whose backstory is Poetic Justice. The theodicy of the Former Prophets amounts to straightforward good housekeeping: people make their beds and sleep in them. But the Invisible Hand has a deft touch. The administration of divine justice involves fitting punishment to crime in vivid and memorable ways.

4. The backstory of the prophetic collections is Anger Management as prophets step into the breach to alternately prod (the community) and placate (the Deity) so as to maintain harmony in the covenant family.

5. The backstory of the Psalms, God Needs Us, has liturgists and priests in a similar mediating position, at one moment prompting the community to turn in gratitude and humility toward God, at the next moment prompting God to be as full of mercy and steadfast love as Moses promised. The dynamic of order and chaos is part of the Prophets and Psalms, but in these sections of Scripture written in poetry we draw deeper water. The problem is not only the chaos in creation; rather, it is the turbulence and ambivalence within the divine nature — the chaos within God — that need careful attention from the community's intermediaries.

6. Proverbs, Ecclesiastes, and Job — the Wisdom literature — invite us to imagine an immense cosmic blueprint upon which the divine design for creation is sketched. In the divine speech near the end of Job, the Bible offers its most complicated theodicy, suggesting that even Leviathan, the dragon of chaos, has a place in the plan.

7. In the final genre historically to emerge in the Hebrew Bible, the apocalyptic literature seen in Daniel and other Jewish and Christian literature from the turn of the era, the Bible retreats from the advances made in the Wisdom literature and turns all of history into a cosmic battle between the forces of light and the forces of darkness. The chaos monsters return in apocalyptic, only now they are members of a universal, invisible conspiracy dedicated to bedeviling the saints at every turn and opposed by angels and archangels locked in *Spy vs. Spy* combat against them.

There is one more backstory in this book. At the end I analyze a minor set of stories that appear in both the Jewish and Christian Bibles about men escaping through windows in order to see if what we have said about the deep biological and theological strata of meaning in stories has any merit. These tales about women who deliver male action heroes from peril are my favorite among the thousand and one narrative structures biblical storytellers constructed to shelter themselves and their audiences from the storms of inscrutable, unscripted chaos.

CHAPTER ONE

The Return of the Chaos Monsters

The Backstory of Creation

God has subdued chaos, just barely.

The Bible's best-known creation account is the narrative that priestly editors used to introduce the Torah in Genesis 1:1–2:3, creation by divine command: "and God said, 'Let there be.'" A different story is told in Genesis 2:4b-25, about creation by divine touch. Here, the Lord God is a hands-on artisan, farmer, and surgeon who molds Adam *('adam)* from soil *('adamah)* that — inexplicably — is already there, breathes into Adam's nostrils, plants a garden, forms the animals and birds, removes a rib from Adam, and constructs Eve from his bone and flesh. The accounts in Genesis 1 and 2 have emerged as the "official" stories of Judaism and Christianity, but there is an alternate creation story alluded to in the Bible.

Priestly theologians buried this story of creation through a competition between the Lord and the dragon of chaos below the surface of their measured prose in Genesis 1, but in the less-constrained discourse of biblical poetry the dragon breaks free. A primordial battle between God and a dragon of chaos, called Leviathan or Rahab, is recalled in these psalms that celebrate creation:

You mashed the [seven] heads of Leviathan. . . .
The day belongs to you; yes, even the night.
    You established the Lights and Sun.

You erected all the boundaries of the earth,
  summer and winter you shaped.   (Ps. 74:14, 16-17)

You crushed Rahab like a carcass. . . .
The heavens belong to you; yes, even the earth.
  The world and everything that fills it, you founded them.
                                             (Ps. 89:10-12)

These texts allude to a story so well-known to biblical audiences that it did not need to be the subject of the first priestly lesson in the primer that became our Bible. Psalmists and prophets assumed their hearers already knew that before time God had defeated the chaos monster, and they did not need to offer a blow-by-blow account.[1]

... in the days of olden times, the generations of prehistory,
was it not you [O Lord] who cut Rahab into pieces,
  who stabbed the dragon?   (Isa. 51:9)

This story of a divine battle at the beginning of time between God and the dragon, between order and chaos, is the first part of the backstory to biblical creation narratives. But there is a second part to the story. As Timothy Beal puts it in *Religion and Monsters,* a survey of chaos monsters from ancient myths through contemporary films: "In the ancient world, as in the modern monster tale, it is difficult to keep a good monster down. They have a tendency to reawaken, reassemble their dismembered parts, and return for a sequel."[2] The Babylonian creation story, identified in the ancient world by its initial phrase, "When on high," *Enuma Elish,* tells such a story and provides us with an explicit narration of matters that the biblical writers left implicit.

The *Enuma Elish*

The *Enuma Elish* tells the story of how Marduk, a storm god and patron of the city-state Babylon, subdued Mother Ocean in primordial times and

---

1. Michael Fishbane observes that there are no "full-scale narratives" of the combat creation myth in the Bible, but rather, "highly condensed epitomes and evocations of these events" (*Biblical Myth and Rabbinic Mythmaking* [Oxford: Oxford University Press, 2003], 64).
2. Timothy K. Beal, *Religion and Monsters* (New York: Routledge, 2002), 18.

then created the orderly world from her body parts.[3] This myth from ancient Iraq in the second millennium B.C.E. explains why we have a world that works. The reason why Wednesday follows Tuesday, the reason why we have a world that is not like some outdated tourist attraction in Chattanooga, the Upside Down House, the reason why we have a world where gravity prevails and dishes do not slide up tables and water does not flow upstream, is this: a long time ago, before time, a god of order defeated the dragon of chaos. We have a world that works because in the very first Western the good guys won, and there is now a cosmic sheriff in town who has locked up all the bad guys.

Who are the bad guys in the *Enuma Elish*? There is Tiamat, a feminine personification of saltwater, and her gang of eleven monsters:

> [Tiamat] gave birth to monster snakes, . . .
> fierce dragons, . . .
> serpents, dragons, hairy hero-men,
> lion monsters, lion men, scorpion men,
> mighty demons, fish men, bull men. . . .
> Eleven on this wise she created.   (*Enuma Elish* 1.134-46)

Tiamat's crew are referred to elsewhere in Mesopotamian literature as "the Eleven." These Malificent Eleven are monstrous hybrids of one form or another — fish-men, winged lions, bison-men, horned serpents — that is, variations on all the centaurs and griffins of ancient art and story, the gargoyles and hairy men of medieval art and legend, and the flying monkeys, X-Men, and mutant turtles of modern children's literature and comics.[4] The very fact that they number eleven, and not the numerically charmed and mathematically soluble ten or twelve, testifies to their wild natures.

The battle itself between Tiamat and Marduk, the template for all subsequent epic showdowns between monster and hero, is dispatched within a mere dozen of the hundreds of lines in the myth incised on clay tablets in cuneiform script and the Akkadian language (4.93-104). At the key moment, Marduk throws a net over Tiamat and hurls a zephyr through the monster's open mouth. When Tiamat inflates like a balloon, the storm god

---

3. All citations from the *Enuma Elish* are from Benjamin R. Foster, *Before the Muses: An Anthology of Akkadian Literature*, 2 vols. (Bethesda, Md.: CDL Press), 1:351-402.

4. For the flying monkeys in *The Wizard of Oz* as chaos monsters, see Beal, *Religion and Monsters*, 104-6.

shoots an arrow into her distended belly to slay her. The Eleven attempt to scatter but are captured. Just like that, reality is stabilized forever.

Or is it? Though Tiamat is slain, her body parts are reutilized to create the world. The recycling of Tiamat's carcass, the creation of cosmic and terrestrial structures out of the limbs and organs of the personified primeval waters, suggests that something indeterminate, fluid, and unstable lies at the substructure of physical reality, that everything fixed might yet sway. Even after Tiamat has been dismembered and eviscerated, watchmen must be assigned to ensure that none of her waters escape (4.139-40). In our final glimpse of Tiamat in the *Enuma Elish* she is "far off, distant forever" (7.134), but even as she ebbs from view, we have the unsettling sense that Mother Ocean might still flow back toward shore. Beal comments on the ambivalent role of the chaos monsters in creation: "The survival of the world . . . depends on the creator god Marduk defeating [Tiamat] and keeping her from returning. On the other hand, [the chaos] that threatens cosmic and political order is also the source of that order."[5] Chaos threatens order, yet the ordered world was constructed when the liquid, chunky mash of chaos was poured into forms. Chaos is the raw material of creation.

Marduk does not destroy the Eleven; rather, they are imprisoned and bound with chains. The imprisonment, but not the obliteration, of the chaos monsters suggests that a healthy world consists of checked raw energy. But chaos cannot be erased because to do so would eliminate change, novelty, drama, or conflict. No sand, no pearl. The Eleven are on leashes at the end of the myth, tied to Marduk's feet (5.72-73), but, presumably, they can still snarl, bare their fangs, and flap their gills. In other Mesopotamian literature and art, the Eleven frequently appear as guardians of the very order they had opposed in the *Enuma Elish*. As such, they are the avatars of all the hybrid superheroes of comic books: that subset of chaos monsters whom cultures depend on to protect them from alien monsters and new eruptions of personified chaos.

So, then, we have the foundation for the longest-running serial in the matinee of literary history: the Return of the Chaos Monsters. The griffins and centaurs and the Godzillas and Draculas, every so often, usually at the beginning of the story or film, escape from their cages and reconstitute their hideous symmetries, and heroes have to spend the rest of the story getting them back into the abyss from which they crawled out.

5. Beal, *Religion and Monsters*, 17-18.

Creation and the Persistence of Evil

What does this story have to do with the Bible? The Bible alludes to this story in Job 3. But before we parse the opaque poetry of Job, we need to look more closely at the biblical creation story in Genesis 1, guided by the Jewish biblical scholar and theologian Jon Levenson in *Creation and the Persistence of Evil*.[6]

Levenson writes that "the point of [the biblical account in Genesis 1] creation is not the production of matter out of nothing, but rather the emergence of a stable community in a benevolent and life-sustaining order."[7] Levenson is challenging the commonplace assumption that the creation story in Genesis 1 describes *creatio ex nihilo,* "creation out of nothing." This religious doctrine reasonably contends that since God was and is all in all, the only raw material for world-making was the wild divine imagination. The idea of creation out of nothing may or may not be true — it has a kind of inescapability for monotheists — but it is not the story narrated in Genesis 1. The Bible begins midstream; the waters were already there. Creation begins when the *ruah elohim,* "the breath of God," moves over "the abyss," *tehom* (Gen. 1:2).

In Genesis 1, then, the primeval cosmic soup is there from the beginning. Where did the chaotic waters come from? The Bible does not say, and this great question must be added to all the "why's" and "how long's" of our dialogue with God. The shadow of Tiamat (Akkadian *ti'amat*) appears in Genesis, not as a personified serpent, but as instead *tehom,* its Hebrew cognate that means "the abyss." There are dragons, the *tanninim,* in Genesis 1 — they show up on day five — but they are just another phylum within creation and are neither personified nor cast as opponents of order. The biblical story of creation rejects the personifying style of myth in favor of a liturgically cadenced ("There was evening, there was morning"), didactic story that reinforces monotheism.

Levenson writes that "the confinement of chaos rather than its elimination is the essence of creation."[8] Creation in Genesis 1 is not about making things out of nothing; it is about bringing definition and identity and differentiation to the amorphous chaos, the *tohu wabohu,* the "wild and

6. Jon D. Levenson, *Creation and the Persistence of Evil: The Jewish Drama of Divine Omnipotence* (San Francisco: Harper and Row, 1988).

7. Levenson, *Creation,* 12.

8. Levenson, *Creation,* 17.

waste."[9] But the cosmic waters are not obliterated. They are fenced in behind a retaining wall (Hebrew *raqiʿa*), a thin colander-like skydome that holds back the bulk of the water but allows for rain through its perforations. This firmament is our hedge against chaos.

But as the tale about Noah and the flood makes clear, the skydome can spring leaks, and the chaotic waters can return. This does not happen because the monsters have escaped; the priestly writer of Genesis rejects the myth he knows so well. In the biblical flood story, the chaotic waters return because of human trespass. "Now the earth was corrupt in God's sight, and the earth was filled with violence" (Gen. 6:11). This ethical breach compromises the terrestrial defense against chaos, leading to the return of the cosmic waters that had been restrained by the firmament. The violent disruption of orderly life, of harmony (Hebrew *shalom*), leads to the inundation of the world with watery chaos. As Levenson writes of Genesis 6–9, "Therein, humanity's injustice threatens to undo the work of creation, to cause the world to revert to the primordial aquatic state from which it had emerged."[10] The remainder of the flood story charts the reversal of the orderly creation in Genesis 1, followed by the re-creation of the world as the tides of the cosmic ocean recede. Follow the water. "In the six hundredth year of Noah's life, in the second month, on the seventeenth day of the month, on that day all the fountains of the great deep *(tehom)* burst open, and the windows of the heavens were opened" (Gen. 7:11). We are now back to before day one, and so the divine wind must again initiate the return of order, as it did in Genesis 1:2 when the breath of God first began to move over the face of *tehom*. "But God remembered Noah and all the wild animals and all the domestic animals that were with him in the ark. And God made a wind *(ruaḥ)* blow over the earth, and the waters subsided; the fountains of the deep and the windows of the heavens were closed. The rain from the heavens was restrained, and the waters began gradually to recede from the earth" (Gen. 8:1-3). Psalm 104:30 alludes to this primeval pattern of the divine breath animating life: "When you send forth your spirit/breath/wind *(ruaḥ)*, they [i.e., the creatures] are created." On both sides of the rainbow, in Genesis 1 before the flood and in Genesis 8 after,

---

9. For the translation of *tohu wabohu* as "wild and waste," see Everett Fox, *The Five Books of Moses*, Schocken Bible 1 (Dallas: Word, 1995), 13; cf. the Miltonic description of hell as a "dismal situation waste and wild" (*Paradise Lost* 1.60).

10. Levenson, *Creation*, 10.

the stirring of the divine wind is the prelude to the creation of order out of chaos. This leads to the emergence of stable terrestrial life and the re-issuance of the command, first seen in Genesis 1:28, to procreate. "In the six hundred first year, in the first month, on the first day of the month, the waters were dried up from the earth. . . . Then God spoke to Noah, '. . . Bring out with you every living thing that is with you of all flesh . . . so that they may swarm on the earth, and be fruitful and multiply on the earth'" (Gen. 8:13, 15, 17).

The sequence of the plot is clear: human violence threatens cosmic or-der and health. God created a world that works by controlling chaos be-hind a firmament. But the chaos is ever ready to break free from its re-straints, and human trespass erodes the stability of the dam behind which the waters mass.

Awakening the Monster

If one wanted to translate Levenson's observations into the idiom of personifying myth — and I do — it would be that "sin awakens the chaos monsters." I will not attempt to track this story, the Return of the Chaos Monsters, through the ages, but I will mention two contempo-rary examples.

When Janet Leigh's character embezzles money from her employer in the initial scene of *Psycho,* she unwittingly awakens the monster, Nor-man Bates, who later destroys her in a cascade of chaotic water. You may prefer Dr. Seuss to Alfred Hitchcock. In *The Cat in the Hat,* a mother goes out shopping and leaves her two children alone in the house with explicit instructions not to let anyone enter. What happens when they vi-olate her commandment and open the door to the Cat in the Hat? The violation leads to the emergence of the chaos monsters, Thing 1 and Thing 2, and the rest of the story is devoted to putting them back into their suitcase.

This story is as old as Pandora's box (or, in the biblical version, the bas-ket containing "Wickedness," Zech. 5:7-8) and as contemporary as the lat-est slasher movie where teenagers engaging in premature sex fall prey to a serial-killing sociopath on a remote lover's lane. The logic of this arche-typal story is that sin awakens the chaos monsters and leads to the undoing of creation. Ethical structures and liturgical disciplines are among our de-fenses against chaos. By keeping the *mitzvot,* by doing *mishpaṭ* and loving *ḥesed,* humans act as co-managers with God of chaos. Virtue keeps the cosmos structured. Virtue keeps the chaos monsters at bay.

So the song they taught us in Sunday school is true after all: it's love, it's love, it's love that makes the world go 'round.

Leviathan in Job 3

The primary, or at least best-known, biblical snapshot of creation morning is contained in Genesis 1. The priestly author of the biblical account of creation in Genesis 1, which probably achieved its present form during the exile in the shadows of Babylon's ziggurats and temples and in competition with that culture's treasury of myths and panoply of deities, is suppressing the role of the monsters in order to differentiate the Israelite view from the Mesopotamian. But if we enter the darkroom and develop some of the other biblical images of creation, we can see the profile of chaos monsters lurking in the background. The biblical text that is most explicit about the presence of the chaos monster in the snapshot of creation morning, the most candid negative of Genesis 1, appears in the book of Job.

There, in the opening statement of the cosmic legal proceedings in which a pious man sues the Creator for breach of contract, we read:

> "Let the day perish in which I was born,
>   and the night that said,
>   'A man-child is conceived.'
> That very day: let there be darkness!" (Job 3:3-4a)

This passage presents a reverse image of creation. Not *yehi or,* "Let there be light," as in Genesis 1:3, but *yehi ḥoshek,* "Let there be darkness" (Job 3:4). Job asks for the tape of reality to rewind, first to the day he was born, next to the very night, forty weeks before, on which he was conceived, and finally to the deep darkness that covered the face of the abyss in Genesis 1:2.[11] If living means burying his ten children and enduring the ravages of a skin disease, then Job prefers that the entire universe revert to the chaotic state he now experiences.

11. Michael Fishbane contends that Job 3 contains a systematic sevenfold reversal of the events of Gen. 1 in "Jeremiah IV 23-26 and Job III 3-13: A Recovered Use of the Creation Pattern," *Vetus Testamentum* 21 (1971): 151-67.

But how does one undo creation? Job continues:

"May those who curse the Day make incantations against it,
     those skilled at awakening Leviathan."   (Job 3:8)

To unleash maximum negative capability, the rewinding of the tape of creation, Job requires a specialist, someone skilled at arousing Leviathan, a flautist capable of charming the primordial serpent from its basket. The clear implication is that once the dragon Leviathan is aroused from her slumbers or freed from her cage, all hell will break loose and creation will start to come undone.

Tracking the Dragon

While we have Leviathan in our sights, let us follow her for a while, drifting in her current through some biblical passages that include the dragon in their backstories. Tiamat, the chaos monster in ancient Iraqi myth, lived in the Indian Ocean, in the Persian Gulf. In Syrian folklore, there is a sea monster in the eastern Mediterranean called Litan, a name cognate to the biblical *Livyatan*, Leviathan, a multiheaded sea serpent (Ps. 74:14). The Greeks called this creature Hydra.

What kind of whale or dugong or manatee was out there in the eastern Mediterranean that inspired all this lore? Some kind of sea monster was rumored to roam right off the coast of Joppa, near what is now Tel Aviv.[12] The Greek hero Perseus came across the natives there preparing to leave a maiden on a precipice for the monster to devour. Perseus rescued Andromeda and defeated the serpent. Hercules, so the Greeks said, got into a scrape about the same place, off the coast of Joppa, and was swallowed by a whale but escaped after three days. In the common era, a Christian pilgrim by the name of George was martyred right around that place, ten miles away in Lydda, and people later told the story that it was this George, rechristened "Saint George," who rescued a maiden and slew the dragon of chaos. I am merely telling you stories, fish stories at that, so believe them at your peril.

12. Herman Melville knew all this; see chapter 82 of *Moby Dick* (1851) for allusions to these traditions about Jonah's fish, Leviathan, and Joppa's sea monster. For a discussion in biblical scholarship, see the references in James Limburg, *Jonah*, Old Testament Library (Louisville: Westminster John Knox, 1993), 61.

But all this lore about the whale or sea dragon off the coast of Joppa helps make sense of the story of Jonah. Jonah was swallowed by a big fish that lived off the coast of Joppa. The fish is neither called Leviathan nor does it symbolize chaos in the book of Jonah (though in rabbinic legend, the fish that swallows Jonah leads the prophet to Leviathan).[13] The "big fish" in Jonah is just one more nonhuman creation (the wind, the sea, the worm, the bush, the livestock of Nineveh) or subhuman foreigner (the Ninevites) that exhibits more obedience to the command of God than the legendary Ephraimite prophet (2 Kings 14:25). But with all this ancient eastern Mediterranean lore about the dragon off the coast of Joppa, we cannot help but imagine the backstory of Leviathan under the surface of the waves into which the Phoenician mariners toss Jonah. It tells us something about Second Temple Judahite religious literature that in its version of the encounter of the hero and the big sea creature off the coast of Joppa, the narrative is not about a combat with a dragon but about a prophetic mission to Nineveh. This is diagnostic. Unlike so many First Temple biblical heroes — warriors who arrested the sun in its orbit, shepherds who felled giants, prophets who made it rain, priests who conjured snakes out of staffs — the biblical heroes of the Second Temple period, like Esther, Ezra, and Daniel (chapters 1–6), forged a new model for heroism built from everyday faithfulness, good timing, righteous living, and spiritual tenacity.

In the New Testament, the sea serpent reappears in one of the visions that John the Revelator saw from the eastern Mediterranean island of Patmos, visions about a final battle, Chaos's Last Stand. John describes a great red dragon with seven heads (Rev. 12:3). If the initial story in the Bible was far away from the *Enuma Elish* with its chaos monsters doing combat with a divine hero, the final story in the Bible is much closer. The red dragon enacts what Beal calls a "chaogony," the struggle of chaos against cosmos.[14] Beal writes, "[The dragon] sweeps down stars" with its tail (Rev. 12:4) and the "primordial flood waters pour forth from its belly" (Rev. 12:15).[15]

We will have much more to say about the book of Revelation when we discuss the world's first conspiracy theory in our chapter on the backstory of biblical apocalyptic literature. Here, we note the pattern of the monster's initial defeat and subsequent return. "Then I saw an angel coming down

13. Beal, *Religion and Monsters*, 69.
14. Beal, *Religion and Monsters*, 41, 77.
15. Beal, *Religion and Monsters*, 77.

from heaven, holding in his hand the key to the bottomless pit and a great chain. He seized the dragon, that ancient serpent, who is the Devil and Satan, and bound him for a thousand years, and threw him into the pit, and locked and sealed it over him, so that he would deceive the nations no more, until the thousand years were ended" (Rev. 20:1-3a NRSV). But we are not done yet. "After that he must be let out for a little while" (Rev 20:3b NRSV). We have seen so many reels of this serial that even in Revelation 20:9-10, where Satan is thrown into the lake of fire and sulfur, the faithful might still worry that the devil is cagily plotting another jailbreak. The chaos monsters always manage to return.

These two texts, from Job 3 and Revelation 20, offer maximum personification of chaos. Many other biblical texts employ this motif, of the reversal of creation and the return to chaos, with far less personification.

Rewind

Job 3 is the Bible's most vivid allusion to the Return of the Chaos Monsters until the red dragon, Houdini-like, escapes his fetters from the bottomless pit in Revelation 20 after a thousand years for a final spree. In the flood story in Genesis 6–9, and in many prophetic texts, creation is undone and chaos unleashed (though not personified) through human trespass. We already saw this theme about how the violence of humans compromised the firmament and led to the return of the chaotic primeval waters in the flood narrative; now we turn to prophetic oracles that have this reversal of creation as their backstory. But in the moralistic jeremiads of the monotheistic prophets, creation starts to come undone and chaos is unleashed through human trespass and the chaos monsters are absent, at least most of the time.

Consider this poem in Jeremiah 4:23-26 where the prophet describes creation in reverse.

> I saw the earth and, look!: wild and waste,
> and the sky and there was none of its light.
> I saw the mountains and, look!: quaking,
> and all the valleys were quivering.
> I saw and, look!: there was no humanity,
> and all the birds of the air had fled.
> I saw and, look!: the orchard was a desert,

and all its cities were laid in ruins
before the LORD, before the heat of his anger.

This oracle, composed at the time of the Babylonian assault on Judah and Jerusalem around 600 B.C.E., portrays this crisis as an undoing of creation. Jeremiah's poem takes us through creation week, uncreating the world one day at a time. We can almost "see" — the dominant verb in Genesis 1 and Jeremiah 4 — the bitter scenario of Job 3 played out one day at a time. In the initial line of Jeremiah's oracle, we are back before day one, with "the earth without form and void" (Gen. 1:2): "I saw the earth and, look!: wild and waste *(tohu wabohu)*." Next, the light, the work of day one, disappears: ". . . and the sky and there was none of its light." Then day three is undone, as we return to the time "before the hills in order stood and earth received its frame," as sketched by Isaac Watts in the hymn "O God, Our Help in Ages Past."

I saw the mountains and, look!: quaking,
and all the valleys were quivering.

The disintegration continues.

I saw and, look!: there was no humanity *('adam)*,
and all the birds of the air had fled.
I saw and, look!: the orchard was a desert.

With the final line of the poem — "and all its cities were laid in ruins" — we rewind to the primeval era, to before Enoch built the first city (Gen. 4:17).

For Jeremiah, this is what the Judahites' wayward ways and doings (Jer. 4:18) have wrought. Genesis 1, with its comforting refrains ("and there was evening, and there was morning," "and God saw that it was good"), has a musical quality. In this passage from Jeremiah, the score of creation, composed in Genesis one day, one note at a time, is decomposed down the scale, one cosmic day at a time. Jeremiah plays the album of creation backward and hears a doom-filled message, just as supposedly happens in contemporary folklore about the hidden messages in pop records.

Roughly a century earlier than Jeremiah, Hosea had described the undoing of creation caused by violations of the Mosaic covenant.

Hear the word of the LORD, O people of Israel;
for the LORD has an indictment against the inhabitants
of the land.

There is no faithfulness or loyalty,
    and no knowledge of God in the land.
Swearing, lying, and murder,
    and stealing and adultery break out;
    bloodshed follows bloodshed.   (Hos. 4:1-2 NRSV)

For Hosea the ritual and ethical corruptions of his eighth-century Ephraimite society were approaching a watershed: his indictment cites violations of a full five of the Ten Commandments given to Moses on Mount Sinai. Now, note the creation imagery in the next section.

Therefore the land mourns,
    and all who live in it languish;
together with the wild animals
    and the birds of the air,
    even the fish of the sea are perishing.   (Hos. 4:3 NRSV)

The ethical failings of the Ephraimites, according to Hosea, have endangered the entire created order. Here, the logic of Hosea's indictment against the people is that, without using any of the personifying images of chaos as monsters, human behavior that is out of sync results in the demise of all life: "the land mourns, / and all who live in it languish."

Isaiah, the most lyrical of the Hebrew prophets, begins a long poem in Isaiah 24–27 along the same arc — sketching the undoing of creation that results from human trespass — but amps up the rhetorical intensity until his poem ends, like Psalms 74 and 89, with Leviathan fully revealed. The poem begins with a description of an act of divine judgment.

The earth dries up and withers,
    the world languishes and withers;
    the heavens languish together with the earth.

                                                    (Isa. 24:4 NRSV)

Why is the earth losing its dewy freshness? Isaiah explains.

The earth lies polluted
    under its inhabitants;
for they have transgressed laws,
    violated the statutes,
    broken the everlasting covenant.   (Isa. 24:5 NRSV)

28

Once again, the entire cosmos, heavens and earth, hovers dangerously on the brink of the abyss because of violations of "the everlasting covenant." This chain of trespass reverses the blessings of creation week and replaces them with corresponding curses.

> Therefore a curse devours the earth,
>   and its inhabitants suffer for their guilt;
> therefore the inhabitants of the earth dwindled,
>   and few people are left.   (Isa. 24:6 NRSV)

The prophet Isaiah describes a world undone by human sinfulness. Note that the effects of their guilt represent the polar opposite of a world where people "are fruitful and multiply"; rather, the population dwindles and humans are scarce. Then, later in the same passage, Isaiah describes the inundation of the world by watery chaos, recalling the flood story.

> For the windows [of the *raqiʿa,* the firmament] have been opened,
>   and now the substructures of the earth quake.
>   (Isa. 24:18b)

It is as if the enormity of human transgression has led to the inundation of the earth with the waters of chaos just as in the flood story, causing the foundation columns supporting the world to lose their footing. The tectonic plates themselves are compromised; the earth sways and quakes.

We cannot know for sure about the historical background of Isaiah 24–27. The major crisis in the background of most of Isaiah 1–39 was the siege of Jerusalem in the late eighth century by the army of the Assyrian tyrant Sennacherib. Some scholars wonder if Isaiah 24–27 was written in the wake of the later invasion, of Babylon, that led to the exile. One can imagine either invasion of Judah around 700 or 587 B.C.E. being portrayed as nothing short of the return of the primeval chaos. Isaiah's apocalypse keeps building on this mythological premise until it reaches the same degree of personification we saw in Job 3 and Revelation 20 with the chaos monster fully revealed:

> On that day the LORD will punish
>   with his hard and huge and strong sword
> Leviathan the fleeing serpent,
>   Leviathan the twisting serpent,
> and he will kill the dragon that is in the sea.   (Isa. 27:1)

29

Cause and Effect

The above prophetic texts directly allude to the reversal of features of the world created in Genesis: the firmament, the light, the birds of the air, the fish of the sea, humanity/'*adam;* all are damaged by ethical violations. A different catena of prophetic speeches describes an even more fundamental disruption, of causality itself. We begin with Micah's indictment of economic corruption in eighth-century Judah.

> Should I consider that rigged scales measure up,
>   or a bagful of fraudulent weights?
> Her wealthy have a surplus of violence,
>   and her inhabitants converse in deception,
>   and their tongue in their mouth is deceitful.   (Mic. 6:11-12)

After this indictment, the prophet issues the sentence:

> As a result, I am starting to assault you,
>   desolating [you] because of your sin.
> You will eat, but not be satisfied, . . .
> you will put away, but not save. . . .
> You will sow, but not reap.   (Mic. 6:13-15)

The essence of the covenant the biblical writers and audiences saw embodied in the natural world and claimed to have seen etched in stone on Mount Sinai was ethical cause and effect. In a later chapter of this book, we will sketch this theme, a metanarrative about "poetic justice" that dominates the narratives of the Former Prophets and is the basis for the oracles of the Latter Prophets. The definition of an orderly world is one in which cause precedes effect. For life to have meaning, predictable reactions must flow from actions: sowing from reaping, satiety from consumption, prosperity from prudence. But the logic of Micah's indictment, a formulation sometimes referred to as a "futility curse" (cf. Deut. 28:30-31, 38-46), is that human sin has disrupted the very chain of causality.

A few decades before Micah, Hosea delivered a similar sentence on behalf of the divine Judge to the defendant Ephraim.

> I will punish them for their ways,
>   and for their deeds I will reward them.

They will eat, but not be satisfied,
 they will promiscuously couple, but not multiply.

                (Hos. 4:9b-10)

Amos also delineates how human trespass weakens the chain of causality.

Because of how you trample the poor
 and take their grain allotments from them,
the houses of hewn stone you build:
 you will not live in them;
the beautiful vineyards you plant:
 you will not drink their wine.   (Amos 5:11)

But in a later oracle, Amos imagines the Lord restoring cosmic harmony, repairing the chain of causality.

I will restore the fortunes of my people Israel,
 and they will rebuild the ruined cities and live in them;
they will plant vineyards and drink their wine. (Amos 9:14)

Isaiah includes the restoration of the missing link between cause and effect as a feature of God's re-creation of the world following the Babylonian exile.

Look! I am creating new heavens and a new earth. . . .
They will build houses and live in them;
 they will plant vineyards and eat their fruit. . . .
They shall not labor in vain.   (Isa. 65:17, 21, 23)

Isaiah's vision of the new creation, just like the renewal of life after the flood, results in the restoration of cosmic order and the restraint of the chaos that would disrupt the operation of cause and effect.

A Full End

We have already seen Jeremiah's description of a rapacious military invasion as the return of the primordial chaos (Jer. 4:23-27). Still, for all of Jeremiah's rhetorical excess, the prophet knows that the ultimate fate of the cosmos does not lie solely in the hands of unfaithful humans. God has a stake in creation too. Though Jeremiah sees the fall of Judah to Babylon as inevitable, he ends his diatribe on a muted note of hope.

> For thus says the LORD:
> The whole land shall be a desolation;
> > yet I will not make a full end. (Jer. 4:27)

Decades later, a poet in exile picks up the same theme. As Isaiah of Babylon writes,

> For thus says the LORD
> who created the heavens —
> > yea, he is God —
> who formed the earth and made it —
> > yea, he established it —
> he did not create it to be chaos *(tohu)*,
> > he formed it to be inhabited. (Isa. 45:18)

Though the prophetic view is that God created an interactive universe in which human behavior, for weal or woe, affects the entire ecosphere, the prophets also knew of a deeper magic than the physics of moral cause and effect. Let us consider Psalm 46, a poem that celebrates Jerusalem's deliverance from an invading army.

> God is, for us, a shelter and a refuge;
> > [as if] in straits, an immense help [was] stumbled upon.
> That is why we do not fear: even when the earth quakes;
> > even when the mountains in the heart of the sea shake,
> the waters splash and foam,
> > the mountains shake from the roaring.
> There is a river: its channels gladden the City of God,
> > the sacred dwelling of Elyon.
> God is in its midst.
> > It will not sway.
> God will come to its help when morning breaks. (Ps. 46:1-5)

This psalm was probably written in the aftermath of the same crisis that lies in the background of Isaiah 24–27. The Assyrian army — the forces of ancient Iraq under King Sennacherib — was outside the walls of Jerusalem around 700 B.C.E. The supply lines to the city were cut off. Assyrian sappers and miners were preparing to dig under the walls. The battering rams and engines of the invaders were being serviced to break down gates and break through walls. The scaffolding and ladders were in place to launch men over the walls. The Assyrian imperial army, over the previous thirty years, had had its way across the Fertile Crescent, from the Persian Gulf to Gaza, and now only the little highland state of Judah, with its capital, Jerusalem, remained unconquered. It finally comes down to this. The citadel of Jerusalem, the site of the divine temple, is being stormed. Another temple, in Babylon, had been the site for the decisive battle in the *Enuma Elish*. For ancient Judahites, the world was reverting to chaos.

Something happened next that we still do not understand. The Assyrian army, on the verge of victory, retreated (2 Kings 19:35-36). Scholars speculate that it could have been a domestic crisis that prompted Sennacherib to abruptly withdraw to Nineveh, or that a gastrointestinal crisis decimated his army.

To the psalmist, whatever the effect, the cause was clear. Though the Assyrian siegeworks, platforms, battering rams, and tents are visible from Jerusalem's walls, though their engineers, archers, infantry, and chariot cavalry camp outside their city walls, they will not fear. If this psalm describes the experience of a people under siege as a reversal of cosmos, as a moving backward through creation week, until the very pillars of the earth give way and the whole thing begins to sway — the work of days two and three — then there is a place where, according to this psalm, the Deity, like Moses' sister on the banks of the Nile, digs in and takes a stand (Exod. 2:4). Though the Orcs beat their spears against the ground until the walls of Helm's Deep sway, we will not fear. Day one will not be undone. No matter how long the night, God will come to Zion's help when morning breaks.

Humans are born to trouble as sparks fly upward; their rapacious machinations have cosmic consequences, unleashing the monstrous chaos controlled by the fragile network of Providence. But when the final strand of the cord that suspends the world over the abyss starts to unravel from the frantic clutching and grabbing of insecure mortals, God, according to this backstory, holds the line. There will be evening; there will be morning, the first day, the next day. In the prophetic doomsday scenarios of creation reverting to chaos, we see the loss of geological superstructures, light, flora, fauna, even causality itself. But the first day, when God said, when God spoke, when God storied, cannot be reversed. What is our final defense against unmeaning? The Word, the promise, the refrain, the song. As long as people have a story, there is hope. There will not be "a full end."

CHAPTER TWO

It's Love That Makes the World Go 'Round

The Backstory of Torah

God has given humans an instruction manual for life on planet Earth so they can partner with God in the management of chaos.

The Bible tells many stories. The Return of the Chaos Monsters is the backstory for biblical creation narratives. Even when, as in Genesis 1:1–2:3, the writer rejects the mythological content of this backstory — the waters are not personified as a monster in Genesis — in the name of monotheism, it is this backstory that is being rejected. God made a cosmos, a world that functions, hums, and purrs, through some invention (such as light), but mainly through arrangement, structuring, and separation. God was the sculptor who discovered the form hidden in the block of stone. Creation in Genesis 1 is not so much about making things out of nothing as it is about bringing definition and identity and differentiation to nothingness. The chaos was not obliterated; rather, it was controlled, fenced in, held behind a firmament. Chaos was organized into orderly structures; "everything according to its kind."

We now must consider the backstory of the Torah, of that vast body of material that spans Exodus, Leviticus, Numbers, and Deuteronomy, the books that follow Genesis. We are pursuing the intersection of creation and covenant, of grace and law, of bounty and duty. The exposed backstory is one in which humans, through living in accordance with the divine instructions, in harmony with the patterns that God sewed into the fabric of reality during creation week, act as co-creators of order and co-managers of chaos, with God.

Torah

Torah in Hebrew means "instruction." The Torah, in its most narrow definition, consists of those materials given by Moses on one of two holy mountains: on Mount Sinai (Exod. 19:1–Num. 10:10, including all of Leviticus)
and on Mount Nebo (Deut. 1:1–33:29). These epic tutorials mediated
through Moses bookend the story of Israel's peregrinations through the
wilderness between the exodus from Egypt and the entry into the Promised
Land. Torah can be defined more broadly as the Jewish term for the first
section of Scripture, the five books of Moses, the Pentateuch. In its most expansive conceptualization, Torah encompasses the entire Jewish canon, including the Hebrew Bible and the classics of rabbinic literature. Torah is
above all a process, the ongoing dynamic interaction of the Jewish people
and their sacred texts. The Christian word "gospel" has a similar breadth: it
can describe one of the four primary books of the New Testament — the
structural equivalent of the Pentateuch — or the entire body of truth sacred
to Christians that was revealed or inspired by Jesus of Nazareth.

The Christian biblical scholar Walter Brueggemann notes that our
common translation of "Torah" as "law" can lead to misunderstanding.
"Torah has within it more that is dynamic, open, and elusive than is con-
veyed in the usual Western, gentilic notion of Jewish law."[1] The
mischaracterization of the Jewish idea of "Torah" as "law" grew out of the
polemics of the early Jesus community and its need to differentiate its message from rabbinic Judaism in the first centuries of the common era.
Christianity offered a "new, improved" religious product, a user-friendly
repackaging of the religion of YHWH for persons who were not ethnically
Jewish. In this first century c.e. fracas among reformers of the Israelite religious vision, the Christians maintained that the fullest realization of human aspirations — the sense that there is an ultimate harmony between
the meaning of the universe and the meaning of one's own existence —
could not be attained through ethical performance, by obeying the "law,"
but only through an act of grace. Let us attempt to frame the Christian position on the question of grace versus law in its best light.

The Christian narrative stressed that God has already reconciled humanity, has already forgiven it, has already healed its brokenness, and the
resurrection of Jesus from the dead proved that God could deliver on this

1. Walter Brueggemann, *Theology of the Old Testament: Testimony, Dispute, Advocacy*
(Minneapolis: Fortress, 1997), 578.

promise. Already, alarm bells of credibility are triggered. We have been forgiven? We have been reconciled?

Yeah, sure.

No, that is the beauty of the Christian version of the story of God's deal with humanity, the twist that Norman Vincent Peale would have appreciated, the power of positive thinking. One does not have to huff and to puff in order to attain "the assurance that one counts for something in the world."[2] One can breathe an easy exhalation into it, "just as I am." The Christian twist on the biblical story is that the world is new, and faith means visualizing this and walking around as if peace and justice and harmony are already here. This narrative was not intended to offer an alibi for inactivity. The acceptance of grace — that our ultimate value is assured by our very birth, that the deepest affirmation of personhood is from a transcendent source — was intended to provide a platform of confident identity and hopefulness that would liberate persons to live in a transformed way.

The skeptical view of this is that Christian theology peddles cheap grace, pardon without restitution. And the Christian view of the primacy of grace has been distorted, daily, into ethical complacency or, worse, a smug sense of spiritual enlightenment.

The differences between this and the positions in Judaism and Islam, as I understand them, are very subtle. Judaism would always stress the primacy of divine mercy, not the primacy of human performance. *God created* a world that is "very good," *God called* Abraham and Sarah to embark on their journey, *God spoke* the Torah to Moses, *God loved* Israel and *liberated* it from slavery. Similarly the first two in the sequence of the ninety-nine names of Allah are "the Compassionate One" and "the Merciful One." So Islam also knows the primacy of divine grace over human ethical performance.

Ideally — and I am speaking here as a Christian, so let the reader beware — the Christian contrast between grace and law does not describe a competition between virtues, but a balancing act. This windfall of forgiveness and reconciliation — the idea that the love we feel and experience is merely the runoff from a great cosmic reservoir of charity behind the dam of appearances — should issue in transformed lives. No sooner had Paul issued his great treatises on reconciliation in the New Testament epistles of

2. John Macquarrie, *Principles of Christian Theology*, 2nd ed. (New York: Charles Scribner's Sons, 1977), 342.

Romans, Galatians, and Corinthians, granting exemptions from the code of the Mosaic law, than he was formulating new codes for the boisterous early Christian communities. You cannot have a grown-up major world religion without a coherent ethical code. Creation and covenant, grace and law, bounty and duty are inseparable. A touch of Jewish realism on the role of Torah in this balance between bounty and duty can be seen in the quip of one of my teachers, James Kugel, who said the Christian formulation that "God is love" is absolutely correct, but that such an abstraction "needs legs." The Torah gives the details.

The contrast between grace and law was, understandably, overstated by the early Christians in their intramural squabble with the Pharisees. In Jewish thought, "Torah" was instruction, not law. Torah was flexible, not rigid. We see this in Hebrew Bible allusions to "the laws of the Medes and Persians" that may not be amended (Esther 1:19; Dan. 6:8, 15). The implicit message was that the Torah was not like the unalterable laws of the Medes and Persians; it was not written in stone, even though that is how the story of the Ten Commandments tells it. Torah was always capable of reinterpretation. In the biblical account of the wilderness period, the very words of the Ten Commandments are different in Deuteronomy than in Exodus (cf. Deut. 4 and Exod. 20); forty years elapse in story time and the divine instructions already have new dimensions. When rabbi Jesus reinterprets Mosaic teaching in the Sermon on the Mount ("You have heard it was said . . . , but now I say to you"), he is merely playing the game of Torah by its own rules. The literary masterpiece of rabbinic Judaism, the Babylonian Talmud, is a transcript of debates among rabbis about how to interpret the divine instructions to Israel. The Talmud thus canonizes the dynamic of interpretation: fidelity to Torah is a given, but the actualization of Torah's demands emerges only through the give-and-take of conversation, not all of it polite, about what it means for a people to walk through history with God. A certain rabbi always gets the last word in a given section of the Talmud, as if his interpretation is authoritative, but dissenting opinions and minority views are preserved for later generations to revisit and make alternate meanings from.

Above all, Judaism always understood that the Torah itself was ultimately a gift that enabled its disciples to live in harmony with creation itself. On the eve of the entrance to the Promised Land, Moses summarizes the significance of what had happened forty years earlier, when the Lord had appeared on Mount Sinai with all the Semitic special effects and had revealed the Torah. "Keep [the LORD's] statutes and commandments that I commanded you today which are for your and your children's **good** after you" (Deut. 4:40). Fidelity to the instructions, to Torah, leads to the actualization of the same "goodness" that characterized God's creation of the world as "very good" (Gen. 1:31).

This is the paradox of Torah. There is a way for communities and individuals to live in fundamental harmony with creation, to be in sync with the seasons, to know, in Wendell Berry's phrase, "the terms and tones" of nature.[3] This is what we dearly want and essentially need, though many of us are captive to a consumer culture that manufactures artificial needs and then supplies them to us, for a price. The way into this living core of reality is through obedience to the commandments, respect for the boundaries that separate order from disorder. When religion gets overripe, these structures too rigid, they defeat themselves and harm life. But when these structures are healthy, they serve as "the wise restraints that make us free," and they promote the harmony, the *shalom,* of living things.

But what of the details that Professor Kugel talked about, those legs that propel platitudes toward practical realities? There are 613 separate commandments enumerated by Jewish tradition in the Torah. The Ten Commandments are a more manageable index formulated for popular consumption: you could count them off one by one on your fingers. In three instances in the first century of the common era religious geniuses attempted further reductions of Torah while maintaining its full value, the way that two-fourths can be formulated as one-half without any qualitative loss.

In a rabbinic debate in which he was asked to name the greatest commandment, Jesus summed up all of Torah in two commandments, "You shall love the Lord your God with all your heart, and with all your soul, and with all your mind," quoting Deuteronomy 6:5, and "You shall love your neighbor as yourself," quoting Leviticus 19:18 (Matt. 22:34-40 NRSV; cf. Mark 12:28-31; Luke 10:25-28). The great first-century rabbi Hillel was also prodded to epitomize Torah by a wiseacre debate opponent who had already stumped rabbi Shammai. In the alchemy of the moment, Hillel transformed the skeptic's base question into a single Golden Rule. "On another occasion it happened that a certain heathen came before Shammai and said to him, 'Make me a proselyte, on condition that you teach me the whole Torah while I stand on one foot.' Thereupon he repulsed him with

---

3. The phrase "terms and tones" is from a poem, "Horses," in *The Selected Poems of Wendell Berry* (Washington, D.C.: Counterpoint, 1998), 121. Berry refers to the language by which farmers communicate, in "gee's," "haw's," and more terms than I know, with horses.

the builder's cubit which was in his hand. When he went before Hillel, he said to him, 'What is hateful to you, do not to your neighbor: that is the whole Torah, while the rest is the commentary thereof; go and learn it'" (*b. Shabbat* 31a).[4]

Our textual sources from early Christianity and Judaism include at least one other example. In the noncanonical *Gospel of Thomas,* uncovered in the ruins of an Egyptian monastery in 1945, the disciples ask their master about correct religious practice. "His disciples asked him and said to him, 'Do you want us to fast? How should we pray? Should we give to charity? What diet should we observe?'" (*Gospel of Thomas* 6.1).[5] This is essentially the same question the scribe asked Jesus and the skeptic asked Hillel. More than a millennium after Moses and 500 years after the first edition of Tanakh emerged in the wake of the Babylonian exile, inquiring Jewish minds in the first two centuries of the common era wanted to know, "What should we do with all the details of Torah?" According to the *Gospel of Thomas,* Jesus replied, "Don't lie, and don't do what you hate" (6.2).

My point is that the details are important: the particulars of the *mitzvot,* whether these commandments are denominated in hundreds, tens, twos, or ones, are what makes Jews Jewish, and the Greek Orthodox Orthodox. In my tribe within Christendom, it is our *mitzvot* of baptism by immersion that defines us as Baptists rather than, heaven forbid, those sprinkling Methodists. The particulars create structures that house communities across generations in places they can recognize as home even as the wider world is in flux around them.

The specific interpretation and implementation of Torah are matters for communities to debate and for divines to distill. But the general principle that unites all communities formed by an ever-reformed Torah is the paradox of bounty and duty, that the fullest expression of life emerges only within the bonds of relationship. "The cloud is free," Wendell Berry wrote, "only to go with the wind." The final stanza of Berry's poem "The Law That Marries All Things" captures the paradox.

> In law is rest
> if you love the law,

---

4. *The Babylonian Talmud,* ed. Isodore Epstein, 35 vols. (London: Soncino, 1938-52), 3:140.

5. The citation from the *Gospel of Thomas* is based on the translation in Robert J. Miller, *The Complete Gospels: Annotated Scholars Version,* rev. ed. (Sonoma, Calif.: Polebridge, 1994), 301-22.

if you enter, singing, into it
as water in its descent.[6]

I know that poets are rightfully protective of their words, but Port Royal's gentleman farmer would surely grant a fellow Kentuckian license to substitute "Torah" for "law." And with that amendment, we have a new stanza of liturgy for an old Jewish holiday, Simchat Torah, the Gala, the Carnival, the Festival of Torah, when the Torah scroll leads a parade of worshipers.

> In *Torah* is rest
> if you love the *Torah*,
> if you enter, singing, into it
> as water in its descent.

Covenant

Both great corpora of Torah, the instructions that issued from Sinai seen in Exodus-Leviticus-Numbers and those presented in Deuteronomy as Moses' farewell address to Israel just before it entered Canaan, have been shaped into the literary form of a "covenant." The priestly and prophetic inventors of the concept borrowed political ideas from their time and region and translated them into a theological doctrine. The treaties and agreements that ancient potentates entered into with client peoples — and archaeologists have provided us with many examples of such diplomatic covenants from the late second and early first millennia B.C.E. — provide us with knowledge of covenants in ancient western Asia. A ruler offered protection and benefits to the ruled in exchange for obedience and tribute. The particulars of this exchange were spelled out in documents that enumerated the promises and penalties that bound each party to the other.

Covenants are sacred bonds of mutuality and relationship. "Covenant" is an old-school, old-country, old-fashioned word. It has deep roots in human culture. Covenant goes back to a time when one did not worry about being sued; rather, one worried about being struck by lightning. Covenant goes back to a time when all knew what first-year law students learn: that the words on our legal documents are not the thing that binds us together;

6. Berry, "The Law That Marries All Things," in *The Selected Poems of Wendell Berry*, 136.

they are merely the witness or testimony to oral pledges people make between and among each other. The sacred part of that is that we use the word "covenant" as opposed to "contract" when there is something holy about what we are doing. In covenants, we stretch language to its furthest boundaries: "So help me God," "Till death do us part," "For better, for worse."

Let us consider the implications of viewing the Mosaic instructions in Deuteronomy as a covenant. The book we know as Deuteronomy is the final form of a tradition that developed over centuries. This tradition began in the northern culture of ancient Israel, traced its origins to Moses, had associations with the subculture of priests at the shrine of Shiloh (most notably Eli and Samuel), was championed by the prophetic heirs to this priesthood such as Elijah and Elisha in the ninth century b.c.e. and Hosea in the eighth century b.c.e., and was carried south to Judah after the collapse of Samaria in 722. There it was preserved and augmented with southern, Judahite elements by northern immigrants in the village of Anathoth, Jeremiah's hometown just north of Jerusalem. In the seventh century this body of religious teachings associated with Moses began to be formulated into a written document.

Eventually, by the time this work assumed its current form during the exile, this collection of religious teachings had been shaped into the form of a covenant, the very kind of political treaty that Assyrian and Babylonian tyrants "offered" to their subjects. Deuteronomy in its final covenantally styled form thus represents a sacred declaration of independence from the Mesopotamian superpowers. Israel's constitution was given to Moses by the Lord. The only treaty it recognized was the one granted by the Creator and ratified through the generations by the community.

It took a learned and sympathetic outsider to biblical scholarship, the historian Donald Harman Akenson, to best capture the significance of Israel's covenant.

The covenant in the Hebrew scriptures is a threefold phenomenon, each of the facets being historical in the following sense:

(1) The covenant happened. Whatever one may feel about the accuracy of the details of transactions recorded in the Hebrew Bible, no one can fail to see that the ancient Israelites made a pretty big bargain with someone or something.

(2) The ancient Hebrew polity explained to itself what had happened in language that was historical. In essence, the ancient Israelites

invented historical thought to explain to themselves how they came to be wrapped in the all-encompassing embrace of Yahweh's covenant.

And (3) the biblical explication of the Hebrew covenant became a model for the way future generations and, indeed, future civilizations, explained the working over time, of social cause and social effect.[7]

In other words, if one steps back from the details of this priestly code that its composers contended governed all commerce between the Lord and Israel, one discovers that God created reality to function according to moral cause and effect. The biblical covenant enshrines this universal truth in the specific dialect of the ancient Hebrew language and Israelite religious culture. The covenant proclaims that God is reliable and that the universe operates by causality. As Akenson further observes, this formulation of causality in religious terms allowed the Israelites to plot their fortunes over time along the graph of divine justice, that is, to narrate the story that has become the Bible.

Links between Creation and Covenant

Jon Levenson in *Creation and the Persistence of Evil* writes about the connection between creation and covenantal obedience and draws attention to certain textual correspondences between the initial chapters of Genesis, with the creation account, and the final chapters of Exodus, with the account of the giving of Torah.[8]

Near the end of Exodus there is a description of the tent of meeting, the wilderness structure in which the Israelites, through a priestly intermediary, would encounter God. In Exodus 39, just the kind of scriptural text casual readers longing for stories and moralisms would ignore and never read carefully, scholars have noted phrases reminiscent of the creation story. Note the correspondence between the bold phrases in the following excerpts from Exodus 39 and Genesis 1-2.

And all the work of the tabernacle of the tent of meeting **was finished**; the Israelites had constructed everything just as the LORD had com-

---

7. Donald Harman Akenson, *Surpassing Wonder: The Invention of the Bible and the Talmuds* (Chicago: University of Chicago Press, 1998), 91-92.

8. Jon D. Levenson, *Creation and the Persistence of Evil: The Jewish Drama of Divine Omnipotence* (San Francisco: Harper and Row, 1988), 85-87.

manded Moses. . . . The Israelites had done **all of the work** just as the LORD had commanded Moses. When **Moses saw** that they had done all the labor just as the LORD had commanded, **he blessed** them. . . . So Moses finished all the labor. (Exod. 39:32, 42-43; 40:33)

Now from the creation story:

God saw everything that he had made, and look!: it was very good. . . . Thus the heavens and the earth **were finished** . . . and [God] rested from **all the labor** that he had done. . . . So **God blessed** the seventh day. (Gen. 1:31–2:3)

The writer of Exodus 39 describes the completion of the wilderness tent of meeting in terms that echo the creation account in Genesis.

Exodus 39	**Genesis 1–2**
Moses saw	God saw
Moses blessed	God blessed
the tent structure was finished	the heavens and earth were finished
all [their] labor	all [God's] labor

As Levenson observes, "Collectively, the function of these correspondences is to underscore the depiction of the sanctuary as a world . . . and the depiction of the world as a sanctuary."[9] The tent — and the temple, for which it served as a provisional frontier prototype — is a microcosm of the entire created world, its physical details a creation story written in architecture, its rites fundamental to the functioning of the cosmos. At the same time, the world is a macrocosm of this tent/temple, the ultimate domain where God reigns and creation gathers in adoration.

Another implication of these verbal correspondences between the creation of the world and the construction of the tent is that, in this way, the writer of Exodus 39, in effect, extends creation week to include the Torah, the Mosaic instruction from Exodus. That is to say, to this biblical writer the patterns and progressions of Mosaic instruction are as foundational to the cosmos as the geological structures and biological arrangements of Genesis. To live according to Mosaic teaching and to worship in the tent are to activate the blessings of creation. Furthermore, to live within the

9. Levenson, *Creation*, 86.

borders sketched in the instruction manual for human life, the Torah, is to buttress the defenses that God has erected against chaos.

When the voice of Moses in the book of Deuteronomy exhorts Israel, "Choose life" (Deut. 30:19), it means just this. If you live according to the *mitzvot* of Torah, follow the instructions, walk the path of righteousness, then you will aid and abet life. Choose life, elect life, opt for life, enlist your measure of will and energy in the cause of supporting *shalom*. All initiatives that augment and support the healthy patterns of God's very good creation, every note we sing in tune with that happy chorus begun by the morning stars on the seventh day, is our covenant response, our partnership, our co-creatorship with God. The goal of legging out every detail of Torah, of loving God with all one's being in sacred and mundane dimensions of existence, is to preserve the fragile boundaries that separate ordered and healthy life from chaos and cosmic disintegration. The backstory of the Torah is that as we uphold the pattern of God's creation (as the priests who composed the Torah divined such matters), we contribute to the ongoing viability of this great cosmic experiment called human life. For our world hangs above an abyss by a frayed rope, a rope whose cords consist of faiths made good, loyalties repaid, and promises kept. Every promise we keep, every commitment we fulfill, makes our world more secure. Virtue keeps chaos at bay; virtue keeps the cosmos structured. Love does make the world go 'round.

Choose whatever virtue you want: love, honesty, loyalty, compassion, justice, righteousness, faith, hope, charity; following the Ten Commandments, following the Great Commandment. At one level, they are all the same. But the converse is also true: that sin, that trespass, that inattention to the details, that self-absorbed, distracted, narcissistic behavior threatens the security of the cosmos; sin threatens to undo the structures of order.

The Priestly Way

My main task here is to help you see the big ethical story of the Bible, namely, that humans have been created to be partners with God in managing chaos and preserving the created order. What we do, or don't do, what we omit or commit: it matters. When we uphold virtue, we make the world more secure; when we trespass, we risk awakening chaos and unleashing destruction.

But what about the particulars? Our task has been to expose the backstory of the Torah, which is that God gave Israel the instruction manual for life so that it could partner with God in the management of chaos and in the vivification of cosmic health. For those who seek to be guided by the biblical witness and who find their identity rooted in the faith of ancient Israel, this backstory remains pertinent even if every community and soul is obliged to blaze its own path through this old-growth forest of tradition, debate, and reinterpretation. The biblical prophets did it one way; the biblical priests did it another. Later we will devote an entire chapter to the prophets; here, we consider the priestly style of ethical leadership, that is, of chaos management.

Rather than waiting for people to make a mess of everything, which led the prophet Amos to leave off his sycamore tree pruning in order to accuse a king of neglecting the poor, or the prophet Hosea to make a big allegorical mess out of his family life by marrying a habitually unfaithful woman in order to dramatize the nation's infidelity, what if, instead of social critics reacting, religious leaders took the initiative and structured the affairs of their community so that the boundaries were maintained and healthy structures preserved? This is what the Torah of the biblical priests sought to accomplish.

There will be Sabbaths where the community pauses every seven days for rest and re-creation, gathering for worship in the temple whose cedar panels and arboreal motifs resemble the garden of Eden, rekindling a lost primeval intimacy, and getting a dose of creative energy before returning to the fray. There will be sabbatical years — every seven years, every week of years — in which the fields can rest, and be replenished and renewed, and return briefly, provisionally, to the creative chaos of wildness. And there will be Jubilees — weeks of weeks, the fiftieth year after seven sevens — in which debt forgiveness is granted so that the effects of chronic poverty do not cripple families over generations, and that restore family farms to their clans, and repatriate exiles, so that the inevitable social inequities that accumulate over time do not damage generations and entire local cultures. For the priests, it is as if this rhythm, six beats and a rest, is the tempo of God's symphony of life.

The priestly impulse was to structure community and family life around healthy patterns. The prophetic impulse was different. The priestly arrangements often get out of whack. Priests are people too and can end up coveting all the white meat from the sacrifices for themselves. Prophets then had this assignment: to exhort, remind, perform, sing, and make a lot of noise when these arrangements got manipulated so that they only favored the families who were in charge. Prophets announced that the priestly constitution of Torah only works if those without social standing — the widows, the poor, the stranger, the orphan — receive the same justice as everyone else.

It is through the partnership of biblical priests and prophets that Torah was composed, preserved, and safeguarded against irrelevancy and manipulation through perennial reform and reinterpretation. The process of Torah, this foretaste of constitutional governance, has been foundational for every culture affected by the spirit of biblical law. At Torah's core is a divine invitation for mortals to live responsibly and meaningfully, to partner with the Creator in the maintenance of cosmic harmony. It is as simple as the song: it's love — every free soul's expression of the beneficence that animates it — that makes the world go 'round.

CHAPTER THREE

Poetic Justice

The Backstory of the Former Prophets

*God has enacted the tough love of moral cause and effect in order
to reward fidelity to the instruction manual and to support
management of the chaos.*

Lord Bezek's Big Toes

The short narrative in Judges 1:4-7 about the violent encounter between
the militia of the tribe of Judah and a Canaanite warlord is one of those Bible stories you never heard about in Sunday school. "Then the militia of
Judah arose. . . . And they encountered Lord Bezek at Bezek, and they
fought against him, and they slew the Canaanites and Perizzites. And Lord
Bezek fled, and they chased him. And when they captured him, they cut
off his thumbs and big toes."

That's all there is to this story, but there's a lot going on here. The
prominence of the tribe of Judah in this, the first battle account in Judges,
is hard to miss. According to the book of Joshua, Joshua himself had cam-
paigned in this same region a mere generation earlier and had defeated a
Canaanite warlord named Lord Zedek, a name suspiciously close to "Lord
Bezek" (Josh. 10:1). Joshua wasn't from the tribe of Judah; he was from the
tribe of Ephraim (Num. 13:8, 16). So do we trust the account in Joshua or
this one in Judges? Was it a member of the northern tribe of Ephraim,
Joshua, or the militia of a southern tribe, the Judahites, who defeated the
Canaanite warlord named Lord Zedek — or was it Lord Bezek? — in the

vicinity of Jerusalem? It seems clear that this initial chapter of the book of Judges gives Judah the glory in any battle. The tribe of Judah, King David, Mount Zion, Solomon's temple: the Jerusalem Chamber of Commerce lobbied hard and successfully to spin most of the biblical story its way, as this chapter illustrates.

Also, we see here the typical form of an ancient battle account, with its two acts. In act 1 the battle is joined and resolved wholesale. Judahites defeat Canaanites and Perizzites. In act 2 the retail ledger is opened: Who individually profits from the martial spoils? Who gets the scalps? Biblical battle accounts usually have two parts: the account of the big battle, followed by the account of the pursuit and capture of the enemy leaders.

Still there's something else here in this miniature battle account. "They cut off his thumbs and big toes." Why this particular torture? Its victim, Lord Bezek, himself explains, and offers the moral to the story. "Lord Bezek said, 'Seventy kings, their thumbs and big toes cut off, gathered food under my table. Just as I have done, so God has repaid me'" (Judg. 1:7). The words attributed to the warlord of Bezek do not mention the men of Judah who mutilated him. The Hebrew word translated above as "repaid," *shillam*, is a verb etymologically related to the noun *shalom*, "peace," or, better, "harmony." The larger truth, explicitly formulated in this brief anecdote, is that it is the deity here, not the warriors of Judah, who has restored the cosmic balance and has justified the moral ledger. This larger truth was something the ancients knew; namely, that a punishment so expertly tailored to fit the crime — the amputation of a sadist's digits — could only be the product of divine handiwork.

Psalm 9:15-16 makes this principle explicit, that any time there is an uncanny symmetry between a crime and its punishment, we have glimpsed the signature of the Invisible Hand.

> The nations have sunk into the pit they made.
> In the very net they hid, their feet are caught.
> The LORD is [thus] revealed; [the LORD] has made justice *(mishpaṭ)*:
> the wicked is ensnared by the work of his hands.

Reading the Former Prophets

This single cell of story about Lord Bezek is diagnostic for the entire body of biblical prose narratives in Joshua, Judges, Samuel, and Kings, that section of Scripture known as the Former Prophets that follows the Torah. The principle of moral causality is the backstory of the books of Moses, but it is more vividly inscribed and memorably communicated through stories about poetic justice than through the statutes of Mosaic law based on the principle of *lex talionis*, "the law of like kind," that had dominated the contents of Leviticus, Numbers, and Deuteronomy.

The Former Prophets is Tanakh's treasury of tales. The best known include the battle of Jericho where walls come a-tumblin' down, Gideon and his fleece, Samson and Delilah, little Samuel in the temple at Shiloh, David and Goliath, David and Bathsheba, Elijah and the priests of Baal on Mount Carmel, Elijah and Queen Jezebel, Elijah and the band of angels, and Elisha and his healing of the Syrian general Naaman. All these and dozens more appear in the Former Prophets, world literature's earliest, longest narrative in prose (Homer's narratives are poetry). And they all tell the same story, that the natural and social worlds are governed by causality.

The dominant theological principle of the scrolls of Joshua, Judges, Samuel, and Kings is that God administers justice on the basis of moral cause and effect, rewarding virtue and punishing vice. Though this doctrine is often termed "Deuteronomistic" because it is formulated so often and so memorably in Deuteronomy, it is more properly termed "Iron Age theology," because it can be found outside Deuteronomy and outside the Bible, even in the religious literature of Israel's neighboring cultures such as in a ninth century B.C.E. Moabite text, the Mesha inscription.

When the Babylonians took scores of Judahites into exile in a series of early-sixth-century deportations and when they destroyed the temple in 587 B.C.E., they also indirectly destroyed the unchallenged efficacy of this Iron Age theology. In subsequent decades and centuries, biblical writers such as the authors of Isaiah 40–55, Job, and Ecclesiastes, and various apocalypticists, would reconsider whether moral cause and effect was an adequate explanation for human fortunes. The punishment of the Judahites seemed immeasurably greater than their sins. Second Isaiah suggested that some suffering might be redemptive (Isa. 52:13–53:12). Job subpoenaed God only to have the Almighty explain that the universe is exquisitely complicated and that the divine justice transcends the binary moral categories of "innocent" and "guilty." Qoheleth shrugged his world-weary shoulders and concluded that a misty, vaporous atmosphere of "vanity" inhibits mortals from seeing the divine patterns. Apocalypticists such as the author of Daniel 7–12 claimed that the very patterns that were so opaque to the author of Ecclesiastes were, to the contrary, crystal clear. The times and seasons had been "revealed" (the meaning of the Greek term *apokalyptein*) to them. The apocalypticists came up with a conspiracy theory, which we will analyze in depth in a later chapter: the reason why the chosen people continue to suffer is because a demonic, universal network is dedicated to destroying them at every turn.

The Iron Age theology of the Former Prophets did not die with the exile. Moral cause and effect remained — and remains — operative. (Really, faith in causality is not merely Iron Age theology, it is every age theology. Even the most sophisticated *philosophes* and sophomoric postmoderns assume that if they turn on the coffee machine, a cup of joe will be waiting for them after they boot up their computers and check their e-mails.) This theology is like Newtonian physics, a viable and enduring explanation for the basic operating system, but less useful the farther one moves toward the margins where light bends, time curves, the wicked continue to flourish and the righteous, to languish. The Former Prophets formulated its conservative, traditional Iron Age thesis so securely and persuasively that it endured long enough for other progressives — ethical quantum theorists — to critique and question it, and eloquently enough to explain the quotidian realities, the diurnal cycles of history where the rise and fall of bodies in motion and of souls in moral combat were still recognizably linear, predictable, and orderly.

A moral gravity envelops the narrative world of the Former Prophets, pulling wannabe royal titans back to earth while "raising the poor from the dust" (1 Sam. 2:8). This common story about how "what goes around comes around" would be tediously predictable were it not for a kiss of style. For as the stories in the Former Prophets illustrate, the Invisible Hand has a deft touch, imbuing the science of cause and effect with poetic qualities. What goes around, *that very thing* comes around. "All they that take the sword shall perish with the sword" (Matt. 26:52 KJV). "Whatsoever a man soweth, that shall he also reap" (Gal. 6:7 KJV). Punishments aptly fit crimes. And therein hangs many a biblical prose tale.

This principle is a staple of storytelling inside and outside the Bible. In Latin, it is Dante's *contrapasso*, "suffering in retaliation for." Biblical storytellers employed it whenever they could, but it is better illustrated in works that are wholly fictional such as the *Inferno*, where Dante depicts gluttons gnawed by a growling dog, or schismatics eternally quartered. Biblical storytellers were enormously fictive, but they were not creating fictions. They worked under the constraints of the checks and balances of their audiences' familiarity with specific and general aspects of a shared folk tradition. Biblical storytellers were free to shape closure and uncover parallels, but not to invent condign punishment from whole cloth.

For that reason, most narratives in the Former Prophets lack the full weight of *contrapasso*'s heavy-handed irony. Abimelech's fate — the man who kills his brothers at the site of a stone is himself killed by a falling stone — is exceptional (Judg. 9:5, 53). More common is a lighter touch of poetic justice. The bard seizes upon a telling detail and uses it to frame the story, such as the winepress in the Gideon narrative (Judg. 6:11; 7:25). Initially, a winepress serves as the site where we meet our insecure hero Gideon hiding his grain from invading Midianites. At the second winepress in the story, Gideon's militia slays the Midianite captains, repulsing their advance. The same object, a winepress, though not the same winepress, serves as the starting and finishing line of a grim competition. There are no loose ends in such stories; underdogs triumph and bullies fail, as illustrated through poetic parallels that bring closure.

Reading Landscapes

The landscape of ancient Israel in the monarchical era, the temporal horizon when so many of the Bible's greatest stories from Genesis to Kings were first composed, was littered with abandoned winepress installations, bizarrely shaped rock formations, and everywhere the rubble from ruined walls and cairns. And inquiring minds were irresistibly drawn to the question formulated in Joshua 4:21, "What do these stones mean?"

The rocks and stones cried out (Luke 19:40; cf. Hab. 2:11). Every pile and feature told a story. Few of the ancients were literate; furthermore, access to scrolls and texts, even among the literate, was limited. Visual art was rarely glimpsed, if at all. So what occupied the visual fields and imaginations of people? The pageant enacted anew daily on Mother Nature's stage by the energetic improvisational troupe of fools, knaves, and, occasionally, heroes in the village. Before the emergence of widespread literacy, our ancestors did not read texts; they read landscapes. They read between the lines of the drama played out before their eyes. They drew lines between events, tracing patterns, explaining accidents, telling stories. No stone was left unturned; to the contrary, the random stones were turned into the loaves that humans cannot live without: the Word of God, the Bread of Life, meaningfulness.

That tower of salt protruding from the cliffs of Mount Sedom along the southwestern rim of the Dead Sea (or some other ancient version of a similar phenomenon) becomes Lot's wife (cf. Gen. 19:26), and the accompanying story illustrates the dangers of looking back when fleeing danger, or of disobeying the commands of patriarchs. The remnants of a Bronze Age village becomes the occasion for an Iron Age story about Joshua's victory over and decimation of the town of Ai, which means "Ruin" (Josh. 8:28).

The ultimate expression of this reading of landscapes leads to the birth of Satan.[1] Although the idea of the devil emerged only in the Second Temple period along with the account of the archangel Lucifer's heavenly rebellion, one of its many roots is storytelling about Venus, the evening and morning star, that can be traced back textually to Bronze Age Syria. Venus is visible only at dusk and dawn, and this led to personifying didactic fables about its absence in the divinized royal court of the night sky. The prophet Isaiah of Jerusalem refers to this story in his "taunt against the king of Babylon" (Isa. 14:4):

> How you have fallen from the heavens,
>> Shining One, Son of Dawn *(Helel ben-Shahar).* (Isa. 14:12)

The eighth-century prophet Isaiah of Jerusalem is describing the imminent fall of the king of Babylon where a big shot finally gets his comeuppance by employing a typical narrative pattern, "Pride goeth before a fall"; "What goes up must come down." Isaiah uses a mythological allusion known to his ancient audience in order to intensify the rhetoric; that is, not merely will a mortal king die, rather, it is as if a divine figure fell from heaven all the way to its cosmic polar opposite, the underworld. We can trace the outlines of such a story based on the fragmentary texts from the Bronze Age Syrian city of Ugarit, which include an episode in which a minor deity, Athtar the Strong, seeks to rise above his station and occupy the throne of the sky-god Baal only to fail and be reassigned to authority over

---

1. The most comprehensive and readable analysis of the devil/Satan is by Jeffrey Burton Russell, contained in four separate works: *The Devil: Perceptions of Evil from Antiquity to Primitive Christianity* (Ithaca, N.Y.: Cornell University Press, 1977); *Satan: The Early Christian Tradition* (Ithaca, N.Y.: Cornell University Press, 1981); *Lucifer: The Devil in the Middle Ages* (Ithaca, N.Y.: Cornell University Press, 1984); and *Mephistopheles: The Devil in the Modern World* (Ithaca, N.Y.: Cornell University Press, 1986). See also T. J. Wray and Gregory Mobley, *The Birth of Satan: Tracing the Devil's Biblical Roots* (New York: Palgrave Macmillan, 2005).

the earth,[2] and another in which Shahar, the morning star (the same name used in Isa. 14:12), is listed as one of the children of El,[3] the patriarchal head of the pantheon.

Isaiah may very well not have known either text. They are merely representative of the kinds of mythological traditions that circulated in the biblical and prebiblical precincts of Syria, Lebanon, Ephraim, and Judah. We have the above Ugaritic texts through a mixture of archaeological ingenuity and blind luck. How many dozens of texts like them have disintegrated or lie unfound beneath the soil? How many thousands of stories like these were told but never committed to writing? Nevertheless, the few tales we do have are suggestive of a mythic backstory about the "fall" of Venus — Shahar in Ugaritic and Hebrew — as an astral deity who got too big for his, or her, britches and was banished to the underworld as punishment. When Saint Jerome translated Isaiah's "Shining One," *Helel,* into Latin as Lucifer, "Light-bearer," around 400 c.e., another story was begotten, the story of Lucifer, the fallen angels, and their failed primeval cosmic coup d'etat. Biblical storytellers considered the lilies (Matt. 6:28; Luke 12:27), and they also considered the heavens, the moon and stars "which thou hast ordained" (Ps. 8:3), constellating every random point of light into patterns, into stories.

The Horse's Hoof

Let me tell a story of my own that illustrates, by analogy, the style of storytelling and meaning-making typical of primarily oral cultures such as that of First Temple Israel.[4] It is an account of my adventures in northern Nigeria with a horse, a herd of pigs, and a telltale hoof. A caution is in order before we proceed: there is nothing, absolutely nothing, "primitive" about the oral style of storytelling. Except for a few bookworms and cyberpunks, all humans, whether literate or not, engage in the oral "register" (the term linguists

2. *Die Keilalphabetischen Texte aus Ugarit* 1.6:54-65, in Mark S. Smith, trans., "The Baal Cycle," in *Ugaritic Narrative Poetry,* ed. Simon B. Parker, Society of Biblical Literature Writings from the Ancient World 9 (Atlanta: Scholars, 1997), 154.

3. *The Cuneiform Alphabetic Texts from Ugarit, Ras Ibn Hani, and Other Places,* 1.23:52, in Theodore J. Lewis, trans., "The Birth of the Gracious Gods," in *Ugaritic Narrative Poetry,* 212.

4. The best description of the style of oral storytelling is by Walter J. Ong in *Orality and Literacy: The Technologizing of the Word* (London: Routledge, 1982), especially chapter 3, "Some Psychodynamics of Orality," 31-77.

use for a given style of speaking).[5] In music, "register" refers to the ability we have to articulate in different voices, such as singing in our normal voice or in the "register" of falsetto. Most of us draw from a variety of registers, adjusting our word choices, grammar, and idioms as we transition through our linguistic experience from writing to speaking, from proper English to the pidgins we use with intimates. There are registers — voices — we use inside and outside: inside and outside of the house, academy, church, and palace, and inside and outside of the social groups with whom we identify or from which we want to separate. We are all multiregisteral polymaths, consciously or unconsciously changing our voices according to circumstance and audience. One can write in an oral style (think Twain in *Huckleberry Finn*) and speak in a written style (think Lincoln in the Second Inaugural Address). We can best see the imprint of language registers when they are violated: in written discourse or on formal occasions, the colloquial seems coarse. In oral communication and personal writing, the formal seems false.

One more caution: I intend to draw no special parallels between the cultures of ancient Israel and contemporary Nigeria, except in the myriad ways that these and every other human culture, including those of other places I have lived, such as rural Kentucky, Uptown Manhattan, and the neighborhoods of Greater Boston, demonstrate that we not only use language in a special way when we speak, but we think in a special way as well when we engage the oral register. Here's my story.

It all started when Steve, my housemate and teaching colleague at a boarding high school founded by Baptist missionaries outside of Jos, Nigeria, went on a trip to Yorubaland down south and left me in charge of the school farm. So every day for two weeks I waded into the infernal muck of the chicken coop and gathered eggs, fed and watered the rabbits in their hutches, and wrangled the pigs who were always cagily plotting a jailbreak, massing at the gate of their sties when I opened it to feed them, bolting if they had half a chance to escape. I was also given responsibility for Steve's horse, the nag he had bought on a lark from Mus-

---

5. For the concept of "register" and its application to orality and literature, see Dell Hymes, "Ways of Speaking," in *Explorations in the Ethnography of Speaking*, ed. Richard Bauman and Joel Sherzer (Cambridge: Cambridge University Press, 1989), 433-51; John Miles Foley, "Word-Power, Performance, and Tradition," *Journal of American Folklore* 105 (1992): 285-89. For the application of "register" to biblical literature, see Susan Niditch, *Oral World and Written Word: Ancient Israelite Literature*, Library of Ancient Israel (Louisville: Westminster John Knox, 1996).

lim traders at the great equine auction in Maiduguri, near Lake Chad. The horse was hitched to a post in a field. On the day the horse kicked me in the head (which was also the day I learned never to approach a horse from the rear), I found the horse at dawn with its hoof tangled in the rope. I knelt down *behind* the horse's left rear hoof to liberate it. I awakened a few minutes later, flat on my back two lengths away.

Sorer but wiser, I then approached the horse from its side, where it could see that my intentions toward its hindquarters were strictly honorable, and untangled the rope from its hoof.

Once the horse was free, fed, watered, and tenderly tethered closer to the enclosures of the other animals, I stumbled toward the pigpen. As soon as they saw daylight, the pigs rudely squeezed by me, four of them, out of the gate, a-squeal on their spree. I gave chase. As I rounded the pigpen in pursuit, I noticed the horse was on the ground.

It took several laps around the barnyard to corral the pigs and return them to their sty. And even though the horse was flat on its back, it wasn't going anywhere, so I held tightly to the Gospel plow and stayed on pig duty. It couldn't have been more than ten minutes later, the pigs happily back in their domicile, stimulated by their exercise and fed, that I was able to respond to the fallen horse.

The horse was dead. As I pondered this macabre turn of events based on my knowledge of the equine sciences, I inferred that the sight of that legion of grunting demons scrambling around the corner of the pigpen, running hog wild directly toward it, had scared Steve's horse to death. Now I had a new problem: what to do with a dead horse. By this time rigor mortis was already setting in, the horse's trunk was inflating and stiffening, all four legs were sticking straight up in the air.

I had the students help me hoist the carcass into the bed of a pickup. I set out on a dirt road, through the neighboring village, and drove as far as I could on tarmac that grew ever cracked, bowed, and rutted. Then I huffed and I puffed until I had pushed that dead horse off the bed of the truck into the tangle and abyss of bush that bordered that final stretch of raised road at the end of the world.

By the time I returned to school, I had drawn a crowd of students, faculty, and staff, to whom I recounted my full adventure beginning with the horse kicking me in the head. The school's night watchman heard my story, nodded in sympathy, and declared, "That horse wanted to die."

A week later, Steve returned. "Where's my horse?" I instructed him to come with me. We drove to the end of the road and got out of the truck. He joined me at the edge of civilization where I pointed down into the jungle and said to him, "There's your horse." All we could see was a single hoof, the rear left, protruding like the hand of a drowning man going down for the last time from that ocean of green.

"That horse wanted to die." That sage comment brought closure to the affair and transformed my misadventure into a morality play. The horse had violated the hierarchy of creaturely station by assaulting a human. Vengeance is mine, saith the Lord, and thus the pigs had been commissioned as agents of moral retribution. There were no loose ends; every event was linked together into a chain of causality and the circle of meaning remained unbroken.

The night watchman supplied the meaning, but yours truly (mainly *truthfully*) had to supply the form in order to complete the presentation in the oral style. The horse's hoof offered itself as the frame for the scenario. That motif initiated and terminated the action, and provided the kind of vivid verbal prompt that oral performers working without a script require to remember their lines. Together, form and meaning coalesce to provide yet one more memorable demonstration of the reality of a deity far more engaged than even Robert Browning could imagine: "God's in his Heaven, [*and makes*] all right in the world."

Poetic Justice in the Former Prophets

Let us begin with a survey of the stories in Joshua, the first of the four scrolls that constitute the Former Prophets. Each story of substantial length — and there are four of them in Joshua — utilizes a recurring physical detail, a variation of my horse's hoof, to frame its particular expression of the metanarrative of poetic justice. The book of Joshua contains more than narrative — there are descriptions of rituals, geographic lists that go for chapters at a time, and much speechifying either from the mouth of Joshua or in the voice of the narrator — but we will ignore all that to float in the stream of stories.

We begin with the adventure of Rahab, the Canaanite prostitute with a heart of gold, and the Israelite spies in Jericho (Josh. 2:1-24; 6:22-25).[6] The

---

6. For the characterization of Rahab as a prostitute "with a heart of gold," and more, see

story of Rahab and the spies is divided into two acts: 2:1-14 and 6:22-25. In the initial scene of the first act, the spies "enter" Rahab's bordello (the innuendo is ummistakable, "to enter," *bo'-'el,* is a euphemism for sexual intercourse in biblical Hebrew),[7] and the king of Jericho gets wind of the strangers in town and attempts to arrest them. But Rahab both hides the spies on her roof and misdirects the Canaanite posse away from town.

> Then Joshua ben-Nun sent *(šlḥ)* from Shittim two men, as spies secretly. . . . They went and entered the house of a woman of prostitution, and her name was Rahab, and they lay down there. It was reported to the ruler of Jericho. . . . So the ruler of Jericho sent [men] to Rahab. . . . But . . . she had taken them up to her roof. She had hidden them with stalks of flax arranged by her on the roof. . . . So the men [of Jericho] pursued the [spies] on the Jordan-road, toward the fords. (Josh. 2:1-7)

The same way she manipulates the flax stalks on the roof, Rahab "arranges" everything; she is the single vivid character in a cast of nameless spies, kings, and soldiers. The way she handles the king of Jericho, humanely misguiding him, is as skillful as the way the midwives Shiphrah and Puah had dealt with another bumbling foreign monarch in Exodus (Exod. 1:15-21).

> Before the [spies] settled down, she went up on the roof to them. She said to the men, "I know that the LORD has given the land to you . . . that all the inhabitants of the land shake before you. . . . Now, swear, please, to me by the LORD that you will perform loyalty *(ḥesed)* with me, and that you will also perform loyalty *(ḥesed)* with my family. . . . Give me a token of your trustworthiness." . . . And the men said to her, "Our lives in exchange for yours if you do not report this deal of ours. Then when

---

Phyllis Bird, "The Harlot as Heroine: Narrative Art and Social Presupposition in Three Old Testament Texts," in *Women in the Hebrew Bible,* ed. Alice Bach (New York: Routledge, 1999), 99-117.

7. For *bo'-'el* in descriptions of *coitus* with a prostitute, see Judg. 16:1; Ezek. 23:44; it is also the idiom used for the liaisons between "the sons of God" and "the daughters of men" (Gen. 6:4), Abraham and Hagar (Gen. 16:2), Jacob and Bilhah (Gen. 30:3), and Onan and Tamar (Gen. 38:8). There is another double entendre in Josh. 2:1, where the spies are described as "laying down," Hebrew *škb,* in Rahab's house. The NRSV translation, "they spent the night," misses this. The Hebrew verb "to spend the night" is *lûn,* but our storyteller uses *škb,* a verb commonly used for sexual intercourse, such as between Lot and his daughters (Gen. 19:33, 35), Jacob and Leah (Gen. 30:16), and David and Bathsheba (2 Sam. 11:4).

the LORD gives the land to us, we will perform loyalty *(ḥesed)* with you, loyalty *(ḥesed)* and trustworthiness." (Josh. 2:8-14)

Rahab continues to knowingly orchestrate everything. For the spies, the outcome of the attack is still unrealized ("Then when the LORD gives the land to us"); for Rahab it is a fait accompli ("I know that the LORD has given the land to you"). It is she who proposes the covenant with Israel; she introduces the term *ḥesed,* Tanakh's favorite word for divine loving-kindness, into the discussion and, furthermore, she models it. The very reason *ḥesed* is used so much for divine loyalty in the Bible is because this virtue is that expression of faithfulness that goes the second mile, beyond the call of duty; it is reserved for acts of grace uncoerced and unmerited. In this charming and entertaining reprise of Exodus, this sister of mercy hides these Hebrew males in the reeds (on her roof) and rescues them from death, even before any covenantal terms had been agreed to on the Sinai-like heights of Jericho's wall.

> Then [Rahab] let them down on a rope through the window because her house was on the exterior wall; she resided in the wall [itself]. She said to them, "To the hills go, lest the pursuers get ahold of you. Hide yourselves there for three days, until the pursuers return. Then after that you can go on your way." And the men said to her, "We will be free from this oath of yours which you have had us swear to you unless when we come to the land you have tied this cord of red thread in the window from which you let us down. . . ." Then she said, "According to your words, may it be." Then she sent *(šlḥ)* them and they left. Then she tied the red cord to the window. (Josh. 2:15-21)

Rahab not only midwifes the male action heroes to safety through the portal at the window, she also maternally instructs them about how to survive until they can safely manage on their own. Surely, her words near the end of the above lines ("According to *your* words, may it be") are ironic — a savvy madam's mendacious affirmation of male performance — because it is *her* words, not theirs, that have been decisive throughout the adventure so far.

In the final scene of the first act of the story, that section contained in Joshua 2, the spies are reunited with their warlord Joshua. "They left and entered the hills, and stayed there three days, until the pursuers returned from their pursuit. The pursuers had searched every road and had found nothing. Then the two men turned and went down from the hills and they crossed over [the Jordan] and came to Joshua ben-Nun. They narrated to him all that had happened to them. They said to Joshua, 'Surely, the LORD has given in our hand all the land, for even all the inhabitants of the land shake before us'" (2:22-24).

Rahab is present even here through her words that the spies repeat verbatim to Joshua. Rahab to the spies: "I know that **the LORD has given the land** to you . . . that **all the inhabitants of the land shake before** you" (2:9). The spies to Joshua: "Surely, **the LORD has given** in our hand all **the land,** for even **all the inhabitants of the land shake before** us" (2:24). Furthermore, Rahab's words ("the LORD has given the land to you") function in this battle account as the "oracle of encouragement," the term for the ritual words religious intermediaries offered to combatants on the eve of battle, assuring them of divine support.[8] Rahab's words — not the spies', not Joshua's, not some Israelite priest's — serve as the omen of victory. Once again in our story Rahab speaks for the divine voice.

The second act of the Rahab story appears three chapters later, in Joshua 6:22-25, after a long embedded section (Josh. 3–5) that locates some of the signature elements of Judahite culture — the practice of circumcision, the celebration of Passover, the founding of the pilgrimage site of Gilgal — in the landscape of Israel's initial generation in Canaan. The conclusion to the story lacks the depth of characterization and wordplay of the first act. The spies are dispatched from the main body of the militia to rescue Rahab and her family, which they do before the town is razed. But this anticlimactic ending does not diminish the vibrant storytelling about Rahab's encounters with the spies in Joshua 2.

The casting of a Canaanite prostitute as the hero of this story was inspired. In the biblical world, a prostitute, as Phyllis Bird writes, was "an outcast, though not an outlaw."[9] She was socially stigmatized, but also socially sanctioned; a fascinating and ambiguous social location. Rahab, along with her house built into the wall on the absolute periphery of Jericho, is truly liminal, on the threshold, which makes her the ideal intermediary in the story. She mediates between Israelite and Canaanite ethnic groups, and, as it turns out, between the divine and terrestrial realms. As we will see in the next chapter, liminal persons make the best prophets too.

---

8. For more on the "oracle of encouragement" or "war oracle," see Gregory Mobley, *The Empty Men: The Heroic Tradition of Ancient Israel,* Anchor Bible Reference Library (New York: Doubleday, 2005), 64-67.

9. Bird, "The Harlot as Heroine," 100.

There is no consensus among interpreters about the significance of the red cord that marks Rahab's house for a passover by the attackers. Some scholars suggest that the cord was the bordello's symbol, that the red cord functioned as a "red light" does in Amsterdam. But we do not know for sure, and the parallel is almost too good to be true. What we can say for certain is, it is the kind of specific ("*this* cord of *red* thread") and memorable detail that storytellers love.

The first part of the story (Josh. 2:1-14) is framed by a series of verbal repetitions that bring the action full circle. It begins with Joshua "sending" (Hebrew *shalah*) the spies to Jericho. They travel *(halak)* and enter *(bo')* Rahab's house. At the end of the chapter, Rahab "sends" *(shalah)* the spies back to their comrades (2:21), and they travel *(halak)* and enter *(bo')* the hills outside town. The mention of Joshua in the initial and final verses of the story also brings closure to this first act. Joshua sends the spies on their mission in 2:1 and hears their report in 2:23-24. The second part of the story, Joshua 6:22-25, does not betray the same narrative energy and commitment, though its final line, "and [Rahab] hid the messengers whom Joshua had *sent* to spy out Jericho" (6:25), does give us a final verbal "send-off," a final repetition of the story's key governing verb, *shalah*.

But where is "the horse's hoof" in our story, the physical detail that boomerangs through the narrative to create a focal point for meaning making and a memorable prompt for storytelling? The surface of the story does not offer such a telltale feature to modern readers. But to its first generations of hearers in biblical Israel, the details about the flax did.[10] Flax is a wetland, reedy herb that was cultivated both for oil and for fibers that were woven into linen cloth. The sheaves on Rahab's roof were flax stalks that had been soaked in order to articulate the fibers, and then left to dry on the roof of a house in the arid Jordan valley town of Jericho. The production of linen from flax was probably a woman's industry, as suggested by the description of "the virtuous wife" in Proverbs 31.

> She seeks wool and flax,
>> and works with willing hands. . . .
> She makes linen garments and sells them;
>> she supplies the merchant with sashes.   (Prov. 31:13, 24 NRSV)

---

10. For the details about flax, and their connection to the Rahab story, see Philip King and Lawrence Stager, *Life in Biblical Israel* (Louisville: Westminster John Knox, 2001), 149-50.

So we have another window in this story, a window into the economic life of Iron Age women in Syro-Palestine. Rahab had her own "cottage industry"; in this regard, at least, she exemplified the proverbial virtuous woman. She hid the spies under stalks of flax; the rope with which she let down the spies from the town wall was made from flax; and the red cord she affixed to her window was made from flax. The sheaves, the rope, the cord: all were products of her own industry and ingenuity. Rahab makes everything happen in this story. The flax provides the thread that runs true through the entire fabric of the narrative.

There are three other sizable narratives in Joshua: the battle account of the Israelite attack of the Canaanite town of Ai (Josh. 7:2–8:29), the conflict with the inhabitants of the Canaanite town of Gibeon that ends uneasily but peaceably (9:1-27), and the final showdown of the book between the Israelites and a coalition of five native militias (10:1-27). Each story has its own recurring motif.

The narrative about the conquest of Ai (7:2–8:29) contains three sections. In the first (7:2-5), the Israelites' initial assault on the Canaanite town is repulsed. In the second section (7:6-26), the reason for the defeat is divined through the casting of lots; the warrior Achan had taken forbidden plunder from the previous battle of Jericho. Once Achan and his entire family are executed, the final section of the story (8:1-29) details the Israelites' successful second attempt to conquer the town named "Ruin."

This final section in Joshua 8 has many of the necessary parts for a classic biblical adventure story, lacking only the personalizing touches of characterization that make heroes such as Moses and Rahab come to life along with their stories. Joshua wields a javelin in the story (8:18, 26), but the arms and this man never nurture the kind of colorful bonding that elsewhere ties Moses to his staff, Saul to his spear, and David to his wadi stones. The problem is that the portrait of Joshua throughout the Bible lacks humanizing detail. There is nothing in the characterization of Joshua that is akin to Jacob's chicaneries, Moses' self-doubts, Ehud's left-handed dexterity, Gideon's insecure penchant for oracles, Samson's libido-driven wanderlust, Saul's tragic derangement, David's music and murderous ambition, or Elijah's cranky intensity. Joshua gives speeches, leads rituals, and issues commands, but he never descends from his Mosaic pedestal to reveal any humanizing details.

Joshua does, however, exhibit a measure of shrewdness in the story, by turning the initial defeat at Ai to his advantage. He leads the main force right up to the gates of Ai, enticing their militia to leave the town and chase the Israelites back into the hills, just as they had before (7:4-5). But this time Joshua deploys a smaller, elite band of Israelite warriors north of the town. Once the Canaanites leave their settlement to chase Joshua and company, the special forces enter the defenseless town and the men of Ai find themselves caught in a vise of Israelite forces.

Two physical objects supply the recurring motifs that frame the story's three sections: the gate at the entrance of Ai, and a large mound of stones. The town gate serves as the backdrop for the final scene of the initial, failed attack. "And the men of Ai struck from [among the three units of Israelites] about thirty-six men, and they chased them from **the gate** as far as Shebarim and struck them on the slope" (7:5). A different object, the rock pile erected over the corpse of the miscreant Achan, closes the second section of the story. "And all Israel stoned [Achan] with stones. . . . **And they erected over him a mound of large stones [that stands] until this day**" (7:25-26).

The end of the entire story squares all the rough edges of the stone gate and stone cairn that had ended the previous sections, utilizing the kind of aural punctuation that ancient storytellers enjoyed and their orally attuned audiences expected. After razing the structures of the defeated town, "[Joshua] hanged the king of Ai on the tree until evening. And at sunset Joshua commanded, and they brought his corpse down from the tree and threw it down at the entrance to **the gate** of Ai, **and they erected over him a mound of large stones [that stands] until this day**" (8:29).

In the next story in Joshua (9:1-27), the Canaanite villagers from Gibeon avoid destruction by posing as recent immigrants, donning the garb of itinerants and begging for terms of peace from Joshua. In their pleas, they repeat the clause "We are your servants" (9:8, 9, 11). Israel's leaders, flattered by this deference and fattened by the Gibeonites' food (9:14a), agree to these terms without seeking divine guidance: "The oracle of the LORD they did not consult" (9:14b). The penalty the Israelites must pay for their impiety, cupidity, and stupidity is the loss of the village of Gibeon from their estate. In a final twist, however, the Gibeonites receive their just deserts as well. "And Joshua said to [the Gibeonites], 'Why did you deceive us, saying, "We are from very far away," when you live right in our midst? Now, accursed be you. May you never be severed from servitude, as hewers of wood and drawers of water for the house of my God'" (9:22-23). The Israelites were bound to the covenant they cut with the Gibeonites (9:15) never to harm them, even if its terms were fraudulent. They had sworn an oath by the Lord (9:19), a name they dared not take in vain. But God is not mocked, you reap what you sow, and the Gibeonites were hoisted on their own rhetorical petard. They got precisely what they asked for: perennial survival and perennial servility.

> [The Gibeonites] said to Joshua, "We are your **servants** (*'abadim*; singular *'ebed*)." (9:8, 9, 11)

> Joshua . . . said to [the Gibeonites], "May you never be severed from **servitude** (*'ebed*)." (9:23)

The motif of "large stones," already used in the Ai narrative, is the structural beam that spans the final adventure story in Joshua, the account of the battle between the Israelites and the Amorite coalition (10:1-27). This battle story has the requisite two acts, the first for the main warfare (10:1-15), the second for the capture and ritual execution of the enemy leaders (10:16-27). At the conclusion of the main battle, the Lord sends "large stones (*'abanim gedalot*) from the sky," hailstones, that add to the panic of the retreating Amorite army (10:11). The Amorite leaders then seek refuge in a cave that becomes a prison when the Israelites roll "large stones (*'abanim gedalot*)" against its mouth (10:18), and once the kings are removed from the cave and executed, their corpses are buried under a mound of "large stones (*'abanim gedalot*)" (10:27). The book of Joshua draws attention to such stones all over its narrative landscape, inscribing the same epitaph on each:

> The LORD is [thus] revealed; [the LORD] has made justice *(mishpaṭ)*:
> the wicked is ensnared by the work of his hands.
>
> (Ps. 9:16)

We now turn to the other scrolls in the Former Prophets, to Judges, Samuel, and Kings, looking for examples of poetic justice. With apologies to the Evangelist and good old King James for this pastiche of their rousing rhetorical finale to the Gospel of John, I can only say that there are so many other stories in the Former Prophets that illustrate poetic justice and rely on a physical object, element in the landscape, or repeated image as a prompt for the composer and focal point for the audience that "if every one of them were written down, I suppose that the world itself [and certainly, at least, this single chapter] could not contain the [lines] that would be written" (John 21:25).

There are the monoliths outside Gilgal (Judg. 3:19, 26) that frame the assassin Ehud's solo mission to Jericho where he eviscerates King Eglon of Moab (Judg. 3:12-30). In the narrative about Gideon in Judges 6–8, the telltale object is a winepress. At the beginning of the story we encounter Gideon "beating wheat in a winepress" (Judg. 6:11) in order to hide his grain from marauding Midianites. The second winepress seen at the end of the story is the site where Gideon kills the commander of the defeated Midianite army (Judg. 7:25). The story that began at one winepress with Israel squeezed into the hills and its fields trod upon ends at another winepress with Midian drained of men and resources. "Stones" bracket the action in the gangland morality tale of Abimelech (Judg. 9:1-57). Seeking to inherit the warlordship and patronage network of his warrior father, Abimelech has his brothers executed on an abattoir stone (Judg. 9:5). He ultimately receives his punishment when an unnamed woman drops a millstone on his head from a town wall (Judg. 9:53). King Ahab wanted Naboth's vineyard, the family farm that abutted his summer palace, so badly that his queen, Jezebel, conspired to have Naboth executed on trumped-up charges (1 Kings 21:1-16). Cut down in battle, Ahab's son Joram would die in that same vineyard, repaid *(shillam)* on "the very plot of ground" for which his father and mother were willing to kill (2 Kings 9:25-26). The foolish disciple Gehazi, dumbfounded that his master Elisha refused any remuneration from the Syrian general Naaman whose leprosy he healed (2 Kings 5:1-19), intercepts the Syrian embassy on their way home from Samaria and concocts a story about how, on second thought, Elisha would be happy to receive a token of royal Aramaean gratitude (2 Kings 5:20-24). Gehazi ends up with a gift, for sure, but it is not what he expected: Gehazi contracts Naaman's skin disease (2 Kings 5:25-27).

Such tales — about the pharaoh who seeks to have all Hebrew boys murdered (Exod. 1:22) only to have his own son cut down by the divine nemesis (Exod. 12:29), and Haman, who is executed on the very gallows he commissioned for Mordecai (Esther 7:10) — occur throughout the Bible; indeed, throughout the public library of world literature and the universal workshop of yarn-spinning. Few of these stories bother to add the moralism so deeply inscribed in the pattern-tracing, meaning-making operations of human consciousness that it can go without saying: God is the author of poetic justice.

Divination through Narrative

Divination, supernatural consultation, was a common practice among biblical peoples.[11] Priests such as Aaron (Lev. 16:8) and Samuel (1 Sam. 10:19) cast lots in order to select a party, whether animal or human, for a holy task. Saint Peter led the disciples in casting lots to determine who should replace Judas among the twelve apostles (it turned out to be Matthias, Acts 1:23-26). Phoenician sailors cast lots and determined it was their passenger Jonah who had brought them bad weather at sea (Jon. 1:7). The costumes of Israelite priests included a breastplate of "judgment *(mishpaṭ)*" that contained the divinatory tokens of the Urim and Thummim (Exod. 28:30; Lev. 8:8; Num. 29:21; Deut. 33:8). Their term for divination was "consulting the LORD," and the divinatory objects were manipulated in a process of binary discriminations akin to the parlor game of Twenty Questions: each token representing the appropriate polarity (cf. 1 Sam. 14:41). The Urim and Thummim could have been dice; we cannot be sure. Dice just like ours — cubes of blue-glazed clay with inlaid white spots ranging from one to six on each face and arranged so that the spots on opposing faces totaled the number seven — were found in the remains of an eighth century B.C.E. shrine at the site of Dan in northern Israel.[12]

Divination is common in the Bible: patriarchs received their dreams, priests read their omens, prophets translated their visions, all searching for some sign of what would happen next, for some prospect about what next to do. The vision of biblical storytellers, in contrast, was retrospective. Storytellers extracted divine communications from the chaotic flow of raw, mute experience, drew inferences from them, and translated them into the patterns of narrative. They knew the folk wisdom of the proverb attributed to Mark Twain, "History does not repeat itself, but it rhymes." Tides of exile and homecoming, of divine mercy and anger, of the rejection of firstborns and the elevation of underdogs undulate through the sea of biblical narrative.

Occasionally, uncanny symmetries between what a man, woman, or group sowed and what he, she, or it reaped presented themselves with the force of revelation. More often, I suspect, the operations of divine justice,

---

11. The discussion in this section is similar to my description in a previous work of the operation of poetic justice in Judg. 6–9; see Mobley, *The Empty Men*, 155-58.

12. Avraham Biran, *Biblical Dan* (Jerusalem: Israel Exploration Society, 1994), 199; King and Stager, *Life in Biblical Israel*, 329-30.

mishpaṭ, had to be detected by interpreters as expert in their divinatory crafts as the priests who wore the breastplate of *mishpaṭ.* The primary oracular mediators are neither priests nor prophets but those who sift through the residue of experience, seek to divine its larger meanings, and then translate these into ordered, meaningful, and memorable patterns: storytellers.

CHAPTER FOUR

Anger Management

The Backstory of the Latter Prophets

God enlists prophets to mediate this dynamic partnership upon which the health of creation depends.

We turn now to that brilliant fusion of divination and imagination known as classical Hebrew prophecy, in which a succession of folk performers over the course of two centuries turned God into a poet. The section of the Bible known as the Latter Prophets or Major Prophets contains edited collections of these performances — its peak years between circa 740 and 540 B.C.E. — and it has its own backstory. We have seen the articulation of the covenant in the Torah and Former Prophets as a partnership between Creator and the people Israel. The health of creation, the management of chaos, depends on the mutual attentiveness and harmony of these partners. But if one theme typifies the quality of this marriage — and the marital metaphor has aptly resonated through subsequent Jewish and Christian interpretation (idolatry as *adultery,* the church as the *bride* of Christ) — it is the instability of the partners and the turbulence of their relationship.[1] The Lord may be slow to anger, but often arrives at that destination nevertheless. Israel, representative of humanity, has a kind of bovine intractability in the prophetic literature; it is a stubborn heifer (Hos. 4:16) that instantly strays

---

1. For an insightful analysis of this often-dysfunctional marriage, see Tikva Frymer-Kensky, *In the Wake of the Goddess: Women, Culture, and the Biblical Transformation of Pagan Myth* (New York: Fawcett Columbine, 1992), 144-52.

from the furrow whenever the reins of tough love are relaxed. Can this marriage be saved? The backstory here, best described by modern Jewish biblical interpreters and theologians such as Abraham Joshua Heschel and Yochanan Muffs, is that it is prophets who step into this breach and act as mediators between the partners in this stormy relationship.[2]

What Is Prophecy?

Before charting the backstory for the Latter Prophets, we take up some general remarks about the phenomenon of Hebrew prophecy. We are accustomed to imagine prophetic vision as foresighted, as seeing forward. In common usage, prophecy is about predicting future tribulations, revelations, or football scores. But prediction is not the focus of biblical prophecy. Rather, as Heschel observed, biblical prophecy is "insighted," not "foresighted."[3] Biblical prophecy is insightful; it is about "seeing through." "Then Elisha prayed, 'O Lord, please open his eyes that he may see.' So the Lord opened the eyes of the servant, and he saw; the mountain was full of horses and chariots of fire all around Elisha" (2 Kings 6:17).

The prophet sees through the veil of appearances to glimpse a different reality. The prophet, as in the above anecdote about Elisha, sees a world that is charged with the grandeur of God and glimpses the cosmic realities — here celestial horses and bands of angels — that are invisible to the prophet's peers. Prophetic vision penetrates everydayness to go deeper than conventional wisdom in order to reveal the story behind the story, the baseline behind the headline.

Occasionally, this type of prophetic vision did uncannily foreshadow the future. But this was not because prophets gazed through crystal balls; rather, it was because under the river of time there is another river whose course, cut into the earth during creation week, is foundational and paradigmatic. Tides — of creation to chaos and from chaos to re-creation, of exile and homecoming, of divine mercy and judgment — undulate beneath the surface, and it is by these eternal wave functions that the prophets marked time and announced seasons. We might understand it this way:

2. Abraham Joshua Heschel, *The Prophets* (New York: Harper and Row, 1962); Yochanan Muffs, "Who Will Stand in the Breach? A Study of Prophetic Intercession," in *Love and Joy: Language and Religion in Ancient Israel* (New York: Jewish Theological Seminary, 1992), 9-48.

3. Heschel, *The Prophets*, xxv.

true prophets — and there were plenty of false ones — were those with a sixth sense, not for hearing voices or sensing intangible perceptions (though that is how the ancients told it), but for registering the transcendent reality beneath and behind the surface of the mundane. For the biblical prophets, the Mosaic tradition, the Torah, served as the lens for interpreting the deepest, truest story. The Mosaic Torah was considered to be the instruction manual for human life. Those persons and communities who followed the manual, observing its times and seasons, its patterns and progressions, were in tune with the underlying principles that structured the cosmos, and approached a state of harmony with God and creation, their word for which was *shalom*. Those who lived contrary to these patterns were moving against the grain of creation itself and courted disaster.

This Mosaic tradition can now be identified with the biblical literature of Genesis-Deuteronomy. We cannot be sure how much of this corpus was extant when the prophets were active, and whether this corpus circulated through written or oral media. Nevertheless, this tradition, the core of which came to be known as the Written Torah, offered the perspective that prophets so immersed themselves in it that they could claim to divine the deeper wellsprings of meaning beneath the showy parade of events, the ebbs and flows in God's management of the world.

The Prophetic Literature in the Bible

The prophetic literature of the Hebrew Bible has been collected in a series of scrolls. The contents of these scrolls represent, in the biblical scholar William Holladay's term, "scrapbooks" that include prophetic poems, prose, prayers, hymns, proverbs, and stories.[4] In the Jewish Bible, there are three large scrapbooks — Isaiah, Jeremiah, Ezekiel, collectively referred to as the Major Prophets because of their length — and a fourth group, the Book of the Twelve, also known as the Minor (i.e., briefer) Prophets. The scrolls in the latter set emerged independently of each other — there was never an actual *book* of these twelve — but have been sitting together through the canonical journey for so long that they are often viewed collectively. The combined contents of the twelve — Hosea, Joel, Amos, Obadiah, Jonah, Micah, Nahum, Habakkuk, Zephaniah, Haggai, Zechariah, Malachi — are roughly

---

4. William L. Holladay, *Long Ago God Spoke: How Christians May Hear the Old Testament Today* (Minneapolis: Fortress, 1995), 192.

equal to one of the major prophetic scrolls in length, and as a result there is a scribal symmetry to the second of Tanakh's sections, the Nevi'im, or Prophets: four collections in the Former Prophets (chronologically arranged prose narratives) and four in the Latter Prophets (the collected speech of the prophets).

Former Prophets	Latter Prophets
1. Joshua	1. Isaiah
2. Judges	2. Jeremiah
3. Samuel	3. Ezekiel
4. Kings	4. The Book of the Twelve

We should note that in Christian Bibles, the Latter Prophets section differs slightly but significantly from that of the Jewish Bible. The Christian Bible has cut two books, Lamentations and Daniel, from the third section of the Jewish Bible, the Writings (Ketuvim), and pasted them into the Prophets. Lamentations follows Jeremiah in Christian Bibles because this poetic elegy for a fallen Jerusalem was traditionally attributed to Jeremiah. More significantly, the book of Daniel, a late addition to the Jewish canon consisting of a generic tangle of fables and visions that abruptly shifts between Aramaic and Hebrew and is located among the miscellany of the Writings, is counted among the Major Prophets in the Christian Bible. The Jewish shrub has grown into a Christian sequoia, and the reason is that Daniel's apocalyptic visions peopled by the Ancient of Days, a Son of Man, angelic Watchers, and archangels Michael and Gabriel always remained esoteric in Judaism, an acquired taste for certain sectarians in their desert communes, while in Christianity the apocalyptic mood was always and ever at the center of the movement.

Who were these prophets who are the subjects and supposed authors of the material in the books that bear their names? Above all, we should keep in mind that the Hebrew prophets were performers, not authors. They were not analogous to preachers in morning suits reading jeremiads from prepared manuscripts or notes. They were more akin to poetry slammers, rappers, performance artists, folksingers, Holiness preachers, merry pranksters, and street performers. The biblical prophetic books represent the scoring of this folk music of prophecy. Let me explain what I mean.

We remain indebted to John and his son Alan Lomax for their 1933 odyssey through the South in search of the musical heritage of "the old, weird America," of the ballads and blues of a vernacular oral tradition in danger of vanishing in the wake of recorded commercial music and its national dissemination through radio.[5] Thanks to them, one can find a song such as "The Midnight Special" transcribed into musical notation with accompanying lyrics in their *American Ballads and Folk Songs* (1934). Ever since, countless professional and amateur musicians have read, performed, and mangled this song. But what none of them can do is recapture the power of the performance that John and Alan Lomax witnessed in 1933 in Angola penitentiary in Louisiana by a man in chains named Herbert Ledbetter, "Lead Belly," who transmuted a train's cry into a prayer for release, for all prisoners, for all peoples, for all times.

Let the Midnight Special shine its light on me.
Let the Midnight Special shine its ever-loving light on me.[6]

The Bible contains the lyrics — faithfully and imperfectly edited and transmitted by generations of scribes — of the prophetic bards of ancient Judah and Ephraim, but we are missing their music. We have neither Lead Belly nor Amos; we have the scribes' version, the Lomaxes' transcription. We are missing the dynamism of their performances.

Still, we have this consolation. Thanks to ancient Jewish musicologists, wherever, whenever the book of Amos is read, we have this oracle whose dynamism and Mozart-like beauty survive even the fallible transcriptions of scribal Salieris and the feeble cover versions of countless clerics.

Let justice roll down like waters,
   and righteousness like an ever-flowing stream.   (Amos 5:24)

These lost performances changed the world. They are the products of a subculture of dissent, of a network of social and religious critics and activists who lived in the highlands of Samaria and Judah in the Iron Age and shared an art form, the versification of the divine word. Not everything about this tradition is unique; in fact, the unique thing about the Hebrew prophets is not their mediation of divine communications into poetic

5. For the phrase "the old, weird America," see Greil Marcus, *The Old, Weird America: The World of Bob Dylan's Basement Tapes* (New York: Picador, 2001). For an account of the Lomaxes' work and its significance, see Benjamin Filene, *Romancing the Folk: Public Memory and American Roots Music* (Chapel Hill: University of North Carolina Press, 2000), 32-75.

6. "De Midnight Special," in John A. Lomax and Alan Lomax, *American Ballads and Folk Songs* (New York: Macmillan, 1934), 71-74.

form — the priests at Delphi revealed the divine will to Oedipus in a riddle — but the impact that Hebrew prophecy has had on human culture. Their eloquent demand for "justice and righteousness" to this day animates activism by humanists and theists; their courageous insistence that royal power be checked by prophetic critique is one of the foundations for constitutional government; and their stringent demand for sole allegiance to the singular but complex Ultimate they knew by the name YHWH allowed for the severe religion of ancient Israel to survive intact from the axial age and give birth to Judaism, Christianity, and Islam while so many of its polytheistic peer traditions were eventually undone by their kindly tolerance for assimilation.

The Theology of the Prophets

With all the Bible's tics and stutters, its epic inconsistencies and ethical incredulities, the irony of the rubric popular in Christian interpretation, "systematic theology," is a howler. *Systematic?* The Bible is all over the place, and as Walter Brueggemann puts it, writing about the portrayal of God in Tanakh/Old Testament: "tension, oddness, incongruity, contradiction, and lack of settlement are to be understood . . . as the central data of the character of Yahweh."[7] The Lord is a moving target.

God comes to Moses on Mount Sinai (or is it Mount Horeb?) in the trappings of a mighty storm, then comes to Elijah on Mount Horeb (or is it Mount Sinai?) in a still, small voice, and then, just when mystically attuned, ethically inclined monotheists think it is safe to come outside, God shows up in the whirlwind again in the book of Job. Still, if there is any place where the Hebrew Bible articulates a systematic theology, it is in that classical depiction of the divine personality that Moses from the cleft of a rock overhears the Lord musing out loud, the Song of Godself, on one of "his" rare post-Eden sightings:

> And the Lord passed by [Moses'] face,
> and he proclaimed,
> "The Lord the Lord,
> El the Compassionate and Merciful,

---

7. Walter Brueggemann, *Theology of the Old Testament: Testimony, Dispute, Advocacy* (Minneapolis: Fortress, 1997), 282.

Long-Nostrilled One,
Surplus of Loyalty (*ḥesed*) and Truthfulness,
Guardian of Loyalty (*ḥesed*) to Thousands,
Bearer of Sin and Iniquity and Transgression,
and Apprehender of the Guilty,
Punisher of Sins
of the fathers upon the sons,
and upon the sons of the sons,
unto the third and the fourth generation." (Exod. 34:6-7)

The basic message of the prophets was that of Torah, that God created the world to work according to causality, that moral cause and effect was the rule, that whatsoever a man soweth, so shall he reap. The Lord would by no means clear the guilty.

But the operation of this cosmic moral cause and effect takes place within the parameters of the divine personality, and the Lord is over-whelmingly bounteous and life-giving, "a God compassionate and merci-ful," *'el raḥum weḥanun*. And — not *but* but *and* — this Deity is serious about consequences; without them life would lack meaning. Long they may be, but there is heat in Jehovah's nostrils.

Divine Anger

We cannot proceed without pausing to reflect on the idea of divine anger without prejudice. No matter how foreign or familiar this concept appears to contemporary readers, it was a consuming reality for the biblical proph-ets and their audiences.

Let me say this clearly: "divine anger" transparently is a projection of emotional qualities onto the blank screen of Ultimate Reality. The reality of divine anger was and remains a largely unquestioned assumption of tra-ditional piety. Divine anger is an odious or absurd concept for everyone else, whether they be religious liberals, the cultured despisers of religion, or simply that great unwashed congregation of those who don't give a damn. The idea of a God who throws tantrums and bears grudges seems infantilizing and trivializing. Ancient freethinkers knew this as well as we do. How could the Creator of the universe be diminished or disappointed in any significant way by the feckless thrashing about of the creatures? Consider the complaint voiced to God by the author of the book of Job who here, as in so many other instances, was millennia ahead of his time: "If I sin, what do I do to you?" (Job 7:20). But you cannot have divine love — the projection of a positive human feeling onto Ultimate Reality — without the rest of the emotional spectrum. And many of us have become quite attached to the concept of divine love. This is the great failing of liberal religion, its naïveté and sentimentalism, its inflated rhetoric about the sweetness and light of divine love, its wishful thinking about cosmic beauty without consideration of cosmic horror. But there is a good reason why progressives have bid adios to this Señor, the stern patriarch. It is because the specter of divine anger has been so abused by authority figures happy to control behavior with implicit and explicit threats to send miscreants to the Principal's office. Divine anger is an idea many of us left behind in theological kindergarten.

But at least three propositions worthy of our respect are hidden inside the archaic, folksy, storytelling, personalizing motif of "divine anger," and the biblical prophets cannot be understood unless we suspend judgment and attempt to understand what it was about the Deity that caused them to tremble.

The first is a core article of faith for theists: Ultimate Reality cannot be less than personal. The qualities that make existence emphatic and sublimely engaging — consciousness and identity — must have some relationship to the character of Whatever Is Most Real, to the being who is the fount of existence, the I AM. All expressions of personhood, then, are fair game for storytelling about God. For Bible readers, there is no escaping the implications of Heschel's contrast between Aristotle's doctrine of God and the thinking of the prophets: the Lord is "the Most Moved Mover."[8]

A second truth contained in the idea of divine anger is that actions have *felt* consequences. It is as if the filaments of the infinitely complicated web of causality and circumstance that make up reality have nerve endings that register the pleasures of kindness and the pains of abuse. Though it makes no literal sense at all — the ground crying out when innocent blood falls upon it? — it makes perfect sense in idiom, in song, in story. The entire cosmos pulses and pangs; in Saint Paul's words it "groans" (Rom. 8:22). The Judge of the quick and the dead, the Supreme Justice who oversees the system of tough love that makes life meaningful, feels outrage when the strong oppress the weak. The administration of divine justice is impassioned.

The idea of divine anger performed a third useful function for the an-

8. Heschel, *The Prophets*, 302.

cients. It encapsulated those all-too-real effects that go beyond causality, retribution, and consequence. Life has always been terrifying, uncanny, unruly, and chaotic, and the structure of this biblical image of an angry God, though it doesn't explain why, creates a space where the support group of all persons who cannot win for losing, who never should have gotten out of bed that morning, meets to vent, console each other, and talk about their problems. In short, the idea of divine anger provides language for talking about our perceptions of divine irascibility and moodiness. Go figure; sometimes God heats up and crazy things happen.

In the mid–twentieth century, the German theologian Paul Tillich formulated the phrase "the God above (or beyond) God."[9] Tillich's words remind believers that in Jewish terms, at the heart of monotheistic faith is the enigma of "I am who I am," that in Christian terms, "we see through a glass darkly," and that in Muslim terms, even the ninety-nine names for Allah do not suffice. The God of the cosmos, a universe aeons old and light-years big, is only hinted at in human theologies, however accurately.

But there's no getting around it. Human beings are storytellers and pattern-tracers, and the philosophic formulations of scholars like Tillich lack the detail and color necessary to sustain virtue and give order to our lives. We need stories and personifications. Who sings about "the God beyond God" in the shower or at the grave site? So, provisionally, with fingers crossed, people of faith walk in the light that their traditions offer, happy for the truth and clarity, the consolations and motivations, they receive. This type of storytelling and these types of personalizing characterizations about Ultimate Reality — that God loves and hates, remembers and forgets, cares and ignores, hardens and softens, caresses and strikes — have a kind of energy, the power to inspire courage, tenderness, justice, and hope, that cosmological and philosophic abstractions cannot match. At any rate, whatever its ultimate validity, divine anger was an inescapable reality for the biblical prophets to whom we now turn.

A Prophetic Glossary

Before turning to biblical examples of prophets performing the mediating function, we must define four key Hebrew terms that show up again and again in the prophetic literature.

9. Paul Tillich, *The Courage to Be* (New Haven: Yale University Press, 1952), 182.

1. *Shuv.* This Hebrew word means "to turn," and is often translated as "to repent." To turn, to repent, means to perform an about-face, to change direction. It is important to retain the concrete sense of the Hebrew, "to turn," when we encounter *shuv* in the Prophets. The histrionics and psychological qualities many associate with "repentance" in revivalistic expressions of religion are absent from the Hebrew. It refers to a change in behavior, not to a chest-beating sojourn on the anxious bench.

2. *Ḥesed.* The semantic range of this word spans a catalogue of virtues, from "love" to "mercy" to "loyalty." *Ḥesed* once denoted "loyalty" or some version of virtuous relations toward members of one's group, and on many occasions in the Bible it means just that: acting like a *mensch,* delivering on promises, doing the right thing (e.g., Gen. 47:29). But often there is something more in the act of *ḥesed* than what is expected among family members or owed to covenant partners. In such instances, there is something surprising about *ḥesed;* it is virtue extended beyond the clan and initiated before there is any social contract (e.g., Josh. 2:12, 14). It becomes Tanakh's favorite adjective for God because God's beneficence toward creation is uncoerced, undeserved, and goes beyond the letter of the contract. Traditionally, in English Bibles, it takes two words to adequately translate *ḥesed:* "steadfast love" or "loving-kindness." That's as it should be, because there is something about *ḥesed,* virtue-squared, that is magnanimous.

3. *Mishpaṭ u-tzedaqah.* This is a phrase, literally, "justice [*mishpaṭ*] and [*u-*] righteousness [*tzedaqah*]." Each word has its own depths, but what is most interesting is the conjunction of the two. The political platform of the classical Hebrew prophets was "justice and righteousness," *mishpaṭ u-tzedaqah,* a phrase the Israeli biblical scholar Moshe Weinfeld has demonstrated means "care for the poor" (cf. Amos 5:18-24; Mic. 6:6-8; Isa. 1:10-17).[10]

For the prophets, the truest measure of societal health was simply, as one inspired heir to the classical prophets, Jesus of Nazareth, put it in Matthew 25:45, the way society treated "the least of these," the widow, the stranger, the orphan, the prisoner, the disabled. In the words of Heschel, the prophet registered "the secret obscenity of sheer unfairness, the unnoticed malignancy of established patterns of indifference. . . . The prophet's ear perceive[d] the silent sigh."[11]

4. *Nḥm.* These are the consonants of a word that, depending on its

---

10. Moshe Weinfeld, *Social Justice in Ancient Israel and in the Ancient Near East* (Jerusalem: Magnes, 1995), 25-44.

11. Heschel, *The Prophets,* 11.

vowels, has different meanings, but always has something to do with a change of affect, a transition along the emotional spectrum from one pole to the other. Most often in the prophetic literature, this verb describes an emotional transition within God, a mood swing of the pendulum between the poles of anger and calm. The verb has two potential aspects: *nhm* can be experienced by its subject (the Hebrew Niphal form), and *nhm* can be extended by its subject to another party (the Hebrew Piel verbal stem).

In its second aspect, when *nhm* emanates from subject to object, it means "to comfort, to express compassion." In its first aspect, when *nhm* is experienced by its subject, it means something akin to "change one's mind" or "regret." Perhaps the best analogy for *nhm* in English is the special sense of the verb "to move," as in, "I was moved by that performance." We use it to describe effects deeper than intellectual persuasion. *Nhm* has some of this: "to move" in its active (Piel) forms and "to be moved" in its reflexive (Niphal) forms. In English "being moved" is not toward a more aggressive state, a stirring up, although in Hebrew this is possible (e.g., Isa. 1:24). Most of the time, the subject of *nhm* is moved or moves to rest, harmony, clarity, satisfaction. It describes those occasions when God is "moved," emotionally, by the prophets.

Anger Management and the Prophets

And the people were continually complaining in the hearing of the LORD and the LORD heard and his nostril burned. And the fire of the LORD was blazing against them and it ate up the edge of the camp. And the people cried to Moses, and Moses prayed to the LORD, and the fire abated. (Num. 11:1-2)

This theme of anger management can be traced between the lines of the Latter Prophets, but it is best seen in narratives composed during the era of the Latter Prophets in which the two greatest figures from Israel's past, Abraham and Moses, are recast as prophetic intercessors.

Let us begin with the story of Abraham's intercession on behalf of Sodom and Gomorrah in Genesis 18. The Lord, who hears the cries of the oppressed, had become alarmed by the sounds from Sodom and Gomorrah. "And the LORD said, 'The outcry from Sodom and Gomorrah indeed is too much, and their sin is very heavy. Let me descend and see what they have done [to initiate] the outcry coming to me'" (Gen. 18:20-21).

We might imagine that in the bazaar of Sodom, a vender was using a false set of weights. In the village square after dark, a stranger in town had been assaulted by a gang of ne'er-do-wells. The marginal were being neglected. The noise of injustice was so great that it had ascended on high, alarming the divine father of every orphan, the divine kinsman of every sojourner in a strange land. In the ancient personifying style, the story reports that the Lord then sent a delegation, three men — three angels — it says, to observe and report back. And if it was as bad as it sounded in Sodom and Gomorrah, the Lord would punish these settlements on the edge of the Dead Sea.

But in an earlier section of the story, the narrator had paused — the same Judahite writer who specialized in sensuous, humanizing portraits of the Deity molding Adam from clay *('adamah)* in Genesis 2 and savoring the smell of Noah's sacrifice in Genesis 8 — to provide a transcript of the Lord's self-deliberation. The storyteller depicts God thinking out loud. "Then the LORD said, 'Should I be hiding from Abraham what I am doing?'" (Gen. 18:17). If God has entered into a covenantal partnership with Abraham, then surely the Deity owes his agent the courtesy of consultation. "For Abraham is to become a nation great and mighty, and all the nations of the earth will be blessed through him. For I have known him so that he would command his children and his house after him that they would keep the way of the LORD, to do **righteousness and justice** *(tzedeqah u-mishpaṭ)*, to the end that the LORD will bring upon Abraham all that he said concerning him" (Gen. 18:18-19). Abraham's assignment includes "commanding" or "instructing" his descendants in the prophetic curriculum of "justice and righteousness" (Gen. 18:19). So who will Professor Abraham's first pupil be?

When the angelic delegation of fact finders departs toward Sodom, Abraham remains behind and throws the rhetoric of justice (*mishpaṭ* and *shopet*, "the Just One") and righteousness (*tzedaqah* and *tzaddiq*, "righteous") back in God's face.

> And the men turned from there and went to Sodom, but Abraham remained standing before the LORD. And Abraham drew near and said, "Would you sweep away the **righteous** *(tzaddiq)* with the guilty? What if there are fifty **righteous** *(tzaddiq)* in the town? Would you really sweep away and not forgive the place if there are fifty **righteous** *(tzaddiq)* in its midst? Far be it for you to do such a thing, to kill the **righteous** *(tzaddiq)* with the guilty, as if the **righteous** *(tzaddiq)* were

the same as the guilty. Far be it for you, the **Just One** *(shopeṭ)* of all the earth, not to do what is **just** *(mishpaṭ).*" (Gen. 18:22-25)

Abraham here deigns to teach God, the "Just One" *(shopeṭ)*, about "justice" *(mishpat).* Abraham stands ("and Abraham remained standing before the LORD") in the breach between God and Sodom, and intercedes on behalf of the community under judgment. There is an ancient tradition, hinted at in the Hebrew Bible but explicit in early Jewish and Christian literature, of Abraham as "the friend of God."[12] The "boundless audacity" of Abraham's ironic retort and the implied mutuality of the intimacy that permits it are suggestive of friendship.[13] Here, Abraham does not kowtow before the Supreme Social Superior; here, Abraham talks back to God.

Moses also enjoys this privilege. "And the LORD spoke to Moses face to face *(panim 'el-panim)*, just like a man speaks to his friend" (Exod. 33:11). But the privilege is accompanied by a grave responsibility, best seen in the story of Moses' dialogues with God following the incident of the golden calf in Exodus 32. "When the people saw that Moses was taking too long to descend from the mountain, the people congregated before Aaron and said to him, 'Come, make gods for us, who shall go before us; as for this Moses, the man who brought us up out of the land of Egypt, we do not know what has become of him'" (Exod. 32:1).

The people at the foot of Mount Sinai make their golden calf. Before, despite the murmuring, God had never gotten very angry with the people. Here, however, God heats up. The biblical idiom for anger is "to have a hot nose"; the biblical idiom for patience and forbearance is "to have a long nose." From this point in the story onward, God does not have a long nose but a short fuse. Eventually that entire generation will die and only their children will enter the Promised Land. From this point on, Moses will need to act as intercessor and mediator between God and the people. God and Moses even verbally spar over *whose* people they are. "And the LORD said to Moses, 'Go down [to them] for *your people* whom *you brought out* of the land of Egypt have acted perversely'" (Exod. 32:7). But Moses implores the face of the Lord his God, and says, "Why, O LORD, is your nostril flaring against *your people* whom *you brought up* out of the land of Egypt?" (Exod. 32:11).

---

12. James L. Kugel, *Traditions of the Bible: A Guide to the Bible as It Was at the Start of the Common Era* (Cambridge: Harvard University Press, 1998), 258.

13. See Muffs, "Who Will Stand?" 11, for Abraham's "boundless audacity."

There is a curious place in the conversation where God seems to *invite* Moses to restrain the divine anger incited by the act of idolatry. God says, "Now let me alone [as if Moses actually is capable of disquieting the Deity] so that my nostril may flare against them and consume them; and of you I will make a great nation" (Exod. 32:10).

This may be my favorite moment in the Bible. All throughout the Bible, the prophets tell the Israelites to "repent, turn," in Hebrew, *shuv.* Here the supreme prophet Moses must tell the Deity to turn: "Turn *(shuv)* from the ferocity of your ire. Change your mind *(nḥm)* about the evil [you intend] toward your people" (Exod. 32:12). Something incredible happens next. Moses' will, not God's, is done. "And the LORD changed his mind *(nḥm)* about the evil that he had said he would do to his people" (Exod. 32:14).

In olden times, God had destroyed all of humanity except for Noah and his family, and though God had promised "never again" (Gen. 8:21), it seems as if that destructive impulse — the reptilian aspect of Deity — had reared its head again. "Of you," the Lord tempts Moses, "I will make a great nation" (Exod. 32:10), as if every ten generations God could start the experiment all over again with a fresh batch. But Moses will have none of it, and in a later part of the conversation he makes it clear that he has no curiosity about seeing such a brave new world, a utopia peopled by a new, improved Mosaic race. "If you will not [forgive the people]," Moses tells God in Exodus 32:32, "then erase me from your scroll that you are writing."

But no good deed of intercession goes unpunished. In the Torah, Moses is allowed nearly unlimited access to the Deity. Moses receives the Written Torah on Mount Sinai (and according to the rabbis, the Oral Torah as well). Moses enjoys direct communication with God, "face-to-face," *panim 'el-panim,* in one idiom (Exod. 33:11; Deut. 34:10), "mouth-to-mouth," *peh 'el-peh,* in another (Num. 12:8). Moses, the divine "servant," has free rein in the chambers of the stratospheric palace (Num. 12:6) where the heavenly councils deliberate. In the theophany that spans Exodus 33:17–34:9, Moses even glimpses the awesome visual brilliance, the "glory" of the Lord; there Moses sees God's backside (Exod. 33:23) and hears God's song (Exod. 34:6). Yet, the very intimacy Moses shares with God alienates him from his community. With them, Moses must wear a veil (Exod. 34:33-35). From them, Moses receives nothing but murmurs, complaints, endless importunities, and jealous personal criticism (e.g., Num. 12:1-2; 14:2). The problem with serving as an intermediary is that Moses gets it from both sides. Moses serves as the welder's mask, absorbing the divine fury on behalf of Israel in the wilderness, and cannot avoid divine anger himself, when in Numbers 20:2-13 Moses stands accused of the misdemeanor of striking the rock at Meribah with his staff twice (when he was only commanded to strike it once? the episode defies interpretation) and is condemned to end his life a fugitive and a wanderer, east of Edenic Canaan. Crisscrossing the threshold between the Deity and the community, pivoting back and forth to face the community with Torah and to face the Lord with pleas for mercy, in the end this hybrid son of Israel and Egypt belongs nowhere, except for in the breach. With no marker for his grave (Deut. 34:6), Moses dies on Mount Nebo in Lincolnesque solitude while Israel enters the Promised Land with, thanks to Moses' intercession, God still on their side.

Analysis of a *Ménage à Trois*

If there is a single backstory to the writing of this book about backstories, it is the immense contribution of Jewish thought to contemporary biblical theology. We have referred already to the work of Jon Levenson, whose analysis of Torah's story about the fragility of creation and the covenantal partnership of chaos management into which Israel (and we might say, the church or even humanity as a whole) has been invited undergirded our chapters about creation and Torah.[14] In a later chapter, on the Wisdom literature in the Bible, the work of James Kugel, another contemporary Jewish biblical scholar, serves as our foundation for understanding "the blueprint" of the created order.[15] Levenson and Kugel were among my teachers in graduate school at Harvard. The view of the prophets as intercessors, rather than soothsayers, offered in this chapter builds off the work of Abraham Joshua Heschel and Yochanan Muffs. Heschel and Muffs, both of blessed memory, taught at Jewish Theological Seminary in New York, which left its mark on me during the first year of my professional life, when I had the privilege of teaching at Union Theological Seminary across the street. Heschel, a teacher of Muffs, is without question the most dominant Jewish figure in contemporary theology. Through eloquent writing,

---

14. Jon D. Levenson, *Creation and the Persistence of Evil: The Jewish Drama of Divine Omnipotence* (San Francisco: Harper and Row, 1988).

15. James L. Kugel, *The Great Poems of the Bible: A Reader's Companion with New Translations* (New York: Free Press, 1999), 116-25.

personal charisma, and social activism, Heschel brought the perspectives of eastern European Jewish mysticism, Hasidism, into the mainstream of contemporary Jewish and Christian thought.

The genius of seventeenth- and eighteenth-century Hasidism was its distillation of what had been a largely esoteric school and style of thinking, medieval Jewish mystical theology, Kabbalah, for popular consumption and practice among the Jews of eastern Europe. Through their mystical texts, allegories, and codes, the Kabbalists had explored the frontier of the Godhead itself and found it to be multitextured.[16] Their Jewish monotheism was not monochromatic; through the prism of Kabbalah a spectrum of divinity was revealed. The divine cloud was a world unto itself in which various expressions of the divine essence dynamically mingled. These medieval Jewish mystical meteorologists mapped the graded array of divinity that spanned — emanation by emanation, zone by zone — the spheres of reality all the way from the atmosphere of the world to the highest stratosphere of the Infinite. Kabbalah was a heady enterprise for a select fraternity of theoretical physicist-theologians. It took the Hasidic masters of seventeenth-century eastern Europe to bring it down to earth.

The basic story of Hasidism is the role that every Jew plays in the drama of "mending the world," *tikkun olam*. Every act of virtue, of faithfulness to the Mosaic commandments *(mitzvot),* of heartfelt celebration of the Sabbath aids the redemption of the world and the restoration of that divine fullness that ever since the big bang of creation morning remains diffused among the multitude of beings and structures in existence. Before time, the blinding Infinite Light exploded into a billion sparks, a happy accident for us since our very lives are merely infinitesimal reflections of this primeval divine effulgence. But this creation of the many left the One diminished. It is the sacred duty of every person to let his or her little light shine, shine, shine, one good deed at a time, and thus restore the full brilliance of the Light of Lights. According to Hasidism, humans aid in the redemption of God as well as of creation.

I first heard a version of this story from a Baptist theologian, long before I left the cradle of the Bible Belt to matriculate in the green pastures of Harvard University and to learn from Jewish scholars on the academic acropolis of Morningside Heights in Manhattan. At the Southern Baptist

---

16. Two helpful introductions to Kabbalah are Daniel C. Matt, *The Essential Kabbalah: The Heart of Jewish Mysticism* (New York: Quality Paperback Book Club, 1995), and Arthur Green, *A Guide to the Zohar* (Stanford: Stanford University Press, 2004).

Theological Seminary in Louisville, Glenn Hinson, a specialist in New Testament and church history, was our guide into the mystical tradition. Professor Hinson one day told us the story of how he discovered the meaning of prayer while reading *Horton Hears a Who* to his son.[17]

In Dr. Seuss's story, the fate of all Who-ville depends on the volume of the alarm its inhabitants could raise; only when every Who down to little Jo-Jo, a very small "shirker, Quite hidden away / In the Fairfax Apartments (Apartment 12-J)," was enlisted in the desperate epic vocalization could Who-ville be saved. Professor Hinson used this story as an analogy for prayer. He said that God had limited Godself in order to make room for creation. The Kabbalists and Hasidic teachers referred to this as *tzimtzum*, the contraction or reduction of the All that took place in the beginning, allowing for there to be the many. Professor Hinson didn't use the Hebrew terms with us, though he surely knew them. He sketched for us an image of a God who had granted a measure of the divine essence, he called it "love-energy," to all the creatures. In prayer the community emits its love-energies back toward God; together, the marshaling of our widow's mites with the vast-but-no-longer-quite-enough reserves of love-energy God still maintains might just fund a new disbursement of cosmic redemption.

You can see the imprint of Hasidic thought with its emphasis on the mutual partnership of God and humans in redemption in Heschel's and Muffs's descriptions of the Hebrew prophets. For Heschel, the prophet was not primarily a wordsmith, bard, or author, but a mediator who occupied an ambivalent location on the border between the human community and God, "facing man, being faced by God."[18] "In the presence of God [the prophet] takes the part of the people. In the presence of the people he takes the part of God."[19] The classical Hebrew prophets lived in this lonely borderlands, like Moses in Transjordan, urging the community to turn toward the Deity, imploring the Deity to be merciful to the people. "This is the burden of the prophet," Heschel writes, "compassion for man and sympathy for God."[20]

Muffs devoted an entire essay to this mediating role of the prophets who lived on the threshold, betwixt and between.[21] Muffs distinguishes between the prophetic personas of messenger — the role we are most fa-

---

17. Dr. Seuss, *Horton Hears a Who!* (New York: Random House, 1954).
18. Heschel, *The Prophets*, xxi.
19. Heschel, *The Prophets*, 28.
20. Heschel, *The Prophets*, 43.
21. Muffs, "Who Will Stand in the Breach?"

miliar with, announcing the divine word to the community — and intercessor. A true prophet, like Moses or Abraham in the above stories, acted both as messenger and as intercessor.

> The first function of the prophet is to announce the punishment and to call on the people to repent. In this role, the prophet acts as messenger of the Lord. But if the people does not heed the prophet's words and does not mend the "fence" of its moral being, the Lord will come as an enemy through the "breach" [in the fortification wall protecting the town]. The function of the prophet is now to go up in the breach, to build a protective wall, and to prepare for the battle against the Lord. The prophet is like a mighty warrior, but his only strength is his eloquence, the strength of his prayer, which may deflect the Lord from destroying his people.[22]

Let us pretend that this dynamic *ménage à trois* of Deity, community, and prophet could be charted. Here's what it would look like.

1. God and the community begin at peace *(shalom)* through covenant.
2. The community breaks the covenant, and the prophets describe this in two ways, along two axes.
   a. Religious and cultic infidelity (vertical ethical orientation).
   b. Oppression of the powerless (horizontal ethical orientation).
3. God heats up and gets angry. Because . . .
   a. God is a jealous husband (vertical).[23]
   b. God hears the cries of the oppressed (horizontal).[24]
4. God expends anger.[25]
5. God cools down and regains the divine equilibrium.[26]

What do prophets do? It depends on where we are in this cycle.

---

22. Muffs, "Who Will Stand?" 31.

23. "They irritated [God] with their high places, / and with their idols they made [God] jealous," Ps. 78:58; cf. Exod. 20:5; 34:14; Deut. 4:24; 5:9; 6:15; 32:16.

24. "If you oppress [the alien, widow, or orphan], then their cry will come to me and I will certainly hear their cry, and then my anger will flare," Exod. 22:23-24; cf. Exod. 3:9; Num. 20:16; 1 Sam. 9:16; Pss. 34:6; 69:33; Job 34:28; Prov. 14:31.

25. "My anger will be spent, and I will lower my fury on them," Ezek. 5:13; cf. Jer. 6:11.

26. In descriptions of this phase, when God shifts from storm to calm, we often see forms of the Hebrew verb *nhm,* as in Ezek. 5:13: "My anger will be spent, and I will lower my fury on them, and then I will calm down *(nhm).*"

In stage 1, the prophet is merely a member of the community and has no special role. Amos was still pruning fig trees in the groves of Tekoa.

In stage 2, the prophet addresses the community, warning them to repent, to turn around, Hebrew *shuv*, and move back toward the harmony, *shalom*, of covenant fidelity. The prophet warns the community that stage 3, the arousal of divine anger, is imminent if they do not *shuv*.

Once we are in stage 3, the prophet addresses God, imploring the Deity to turn, *shuv*, and seeks to blunt or absorb the divine fury, avoiding or minimizing stage 4.

In stage 4 the prophet turns back toward the community with bad news. The cycle of punishment is now in motion and must run full circle: duck and cover.

In stage 5, the prophet turns toward the community with good news, with glad tidings of great joy, with the comforting message that the divine anger is spent, that God is emotionally stable again.

What is the measure of a supreme prophet? As Exodus 32:14 indicates ("And the LORD changed his mind [*nḥm*] about the evil that he had said he would do to his people"), a prophet who is worth a damn, like Moses, can get you from stage 3 to stage 5 without stage 4.

> [The LORD] had announced that he would destroy them,
>> if Moses, his chosen one,
> had not stood in the breach before him,
>> to turn (*shuv*) his fury from destroying them.　　　(Ps. 106:23)

Intercession in the Latter Prophets

It is time to illustrate this cycle as it is played out in the oracles of the Latter Prophets. In stage 1 of this dynamic interaction among God, the community, and their prophetic mediator, those five minutes every century or so when "the land had rest," the prophet is quiescent as well.

In stage 2, when the troubling sparks of idolatry and injustice inevitably fly upward and threaten to ignite the divine temper, the prophet's conscience is activated and he sounds the alarm: turn around, repent, change direction.

> O house of Jacob,
>> come, let us walk
>> in the light of the LORD.　　　(Isa. 2:5)

Turn around *(shuv),* turned-around Israel, . . .
I will not hold a grudge forever. (Jer. 3:12)

 Rend your hearts and not your clothing,
and turn back *(shuv)* to the LORD your God,
 for he is compassionate and favorable,
long-nostrilled, a surplus of loyalty *(ḥesed),*
 and one who changes his mind *(nḥm)* about doing evil.
Who knows? He may turn *(shuv)* and calm down *(nḥm).*
(Joel 2:13-14)

In stage 2, when the prophet can see the anger (in Kabbalistic terms, the *din,* the emanation of judgment) beginning to stir inside the Godhead, the prophet addresses the community. And the Hebrew prophets were unanimous in maintaining the position that religious rituals such as animal sacrifices were useless in moving God from anger to calm.

Hear the word of the LORD, . . .
What to me are more of your sacrifices?
 the LORD says;
I am not satiated with incinerated rams
 and the fat of beef cattle;
and the blood of bulls or lambs or goats I do not want.
When you come to appear before me,
 who sought this from your hands as you trample my courtyards?
Bring no more empty tribute.
 Incense is abhorrent to me.
New Moon services, Sabbaths, special convocations:
 I cannot abide an empty holiday.
Your New Moon services and your assemblies,
 my soul despises.
They have become a burden to me that
 I am weary of carrying.
When you spread out your hands,
 I will cover up my eyes from you.
Even if you repeat prayers,
 there will be no hearing on my part,
 [because] your forearms are drenched in blood. (Isa. 1:10-15)

The only response acceptable is a turning from violence toward and neglect of the poor.

> Rinse yourselves, clean up;
>> remove the evil of your practices
>> from before my eyes,
> cease to do evil,
>> learn to do good,
> pursue justice *(mishpaṭ)*,
>> lead out the oppressed [from their predicament],
> defend the orphan,
>> plead for the widow.   (Isa. 1:16-17)

This is the consistent message of the eighth-century prophets in Judah and Ephraim: that once God has been provoked to anger by idolatry and injustice, the props and features of cultic pomp and circumstance are only fuel for the fire of the divine choler.

> I hate, I reject your pilgrimage festivals;
>> I find odious your holidays.   (Amos 5:21)

Only the most dramatic ethical about-face has a chance of pacifying an increasingly enraged God.

> Take away from me the noise of your songs;
>> and to the tunes of your harps, I am deaf.
> But let justice *(mishpaṭ)* roll down like waters,
>> and righteousness *(tzedaqah)* like an ever-flowing stream.
>>   (Amos 5:23-24)

Hosea puts it this way, speaking in the guise of the divine messenger:

> For it is covenant loyalty *(ḥesed)* I desire, and not animal sacrifice,
>> and a knowing relationship with God rather than cereal offerings.
>>   (Hos. 6:6)

Neither cereal offerings nor slaughtered calves nor thousands of rams nor myriads of olive oil libations nor (and we hope but cannot be sure that the prophet is merely rhetorical here) the sacrifice of one's firstborn child will mollify the Lord once we reach stage 2 of this dysfunctional family system

(Mic. 6:6-7). What does the Lord require, then, according to the prophet Micah?

> Perform justice *(mishpaṭ)*, and love loyalty *(ḥesed)*,
>> and with the utmost care walk with your God. (Mic. 6:8)

Jeremiah echoed the message of his eighth-century prophetic mentors in his sixth-century parody of Judahite piety. "Do not trust in these deceptive words, 'The Temple of the LORD, the Temple of the LORD, the Temple of the LORD; this is the place!' But if you rectify your ways and your practices, if you perform justice *(mishpaṭ)* toward each other, . . . then I will dwell with you in this place" (Jer. 7:4-5, 7).

Once we are in stage 3, the prophet pivots to address God rather than the people, and implores the Deity to turn *(shuv)*. The prophet seeks to blunt or absorb the divine fury, avoiding or minimizing the terrifying release of the divine anger that awaits in stage 4. The prophet Jeremiah recalls a time when he took his stand in the breach.

> Remember how I stood before you,
>> to speak about them favorably,
>> to turn your anger away from them. (Jer. 18:20)[27]

In the book of Joel, the initial oracle (Joel 1:2-14) consists of the prophet's instructions to the community, delivered in a series of imperatives, "Hear this!," "Wake up!," "Wail!," "Shame on you!," "Put on sackcloth!," and "Observe a fast!" But then Joel pivots to plead to God on behalf of the people: "Unto you, O LORD, I call," and even on behalf of the animals who also suffer the effects of a drought: "Even the beasts of the field pant for you" (Joel 1:19-20). Amos appeals to God's affection for the underdog in two episodes of intercession.

> "My Master, the LORD, forgive, please!
>> How can Jacob stand,
>> for he is small?"
> And the LORD relented *(nḥm)* concerning this.
>> "[The punishment] will not happen," says the LORD. (Amos 7:2-3)

> "My Master LORD, arrest yourself, please!
>> How can Jacob stand,

---

27. Heschel, *The Prophets*, 154.

for he is small?"
And the LORD relented *(nḥm)* concerning this.
"[The punishment] also will not happen," says the Master,
  the LORD.   (Amos 7:5-6)

The scroll of Micah ends on a crescendo of prophetic intercession as Micah calls on God to exemplify the first half of the classic formulation of the divine personality in Exodus 34:6-7, and to stop short of its avenging second half.

Who is a Deity like you?
Bearing sin
 and passing over transgression
 to the remnant of his possession.
He does not forever harden his anger,
 but he delights in displaying unmerited loyalty *(ḥesed)*.
He will again have compassion on us;
 he will tread on our iniquities.
You will cast into the depths of the sea
 their sins.
You will offer truthfulness to Jacob
 and unmerited loyalty *(ḥesed)* to Abraham,
as you swore to our ancestors
 from olden days.   (Mic. 7:18-20)

The Kabbalists had their own code for this, and though it was formulated centuries after the era of classical prophecy, it is true to its spirit. They imagined the divine attributes of judgment and mercy, *din* and *ḥesed*, as adjoining chambers within the temple of the divine interiority. The prophet's rhetorical massaging — Have mercy! Remember your promises to the ancestors! They are your people! — could stimulate the movement of God from one pole to the other.

There are occasions when prophets are banned from intercession, an indirect affirmation of their mediating efficacy. Jeremiah is commanded not to intercede: "The LORD said to me, 'Do not pray for something good on behalf of this people'" (Jer. 14:11), but the prophet immediately sighs for them nonetheless: "But I said, 'Oh Master LORD'" (Jer. 14:13).[28] At another

---

28. Ezekiel is also commanded to keep silence, to eschew oracles of judgment against Judah and pleas for mercy to the Lord, until the ordained punishment, the destruction of the temple and of Jerusalem, has run its course (Ezek. 24:25-27).

place in the ongoing trauma of Jeremiah's emotionally charged prophetic dialogue with God (in Jeremiah, the agency of contact is neither mouth-to-mouth nor face-to-face, but heart-to-heart or guts-to-guts), the Lord announces that even the pleas from the greatest prophetic heroes of Jeremiah's northern heritage would be ignored in this crisis on the eve of exile. "And the LORD said to me: Even if Moses and Samuel were to stand before me, I would have no feeling for this people" (Jer. 15:1).[29]

Worthless prophets are those who do not honor the task of intercession, who do not interpose themselves between an enraged Deity bent on punishment and the community threatened by the advance of the divine nemesis. "Like jackals [scurrying] among ruins are your prophets, O Israel. [They] did not go up into the breaches, they did not repair the wall on behalf of the house of Israel so that it would withstand the battle on the day of the LORD" (Ezek. 13:4-5). Muffs draws our attention to another passage in Ezekiel that utilizes the same image of the prophet as mason as it voices the Deity's regret about the dire consequences that ensue when prophetic mediation is absent.[30] "I searched among them for a man to repair the wall, a man to stand in the breach before me on behalf of the land, so I would not destroy it. But I couldn't find one. So I poured out on them my curse, with the fire of my rage, I consumed them. I gave them their conduct back on their heads" (Ezek. 22:30-31).

This dynamic of prophetic intercession is so essential to the maintenance of the divine-human relationship that if the prophet does not intercede, God may have to act out all the parts Godself. Against the backdrop of the dynamic interplay of Kabbalistic *din* and *ḥesed*, Muffs writes: "But what happens if an intercessor does not arise to . . . stand in the breach with his prayer, to deflect the anger of the Lord from destroying? According to the rabbis, the Holy One, Blessed Be He, rises from His chair of strict justice and goes to sit upon His chair of mercy. It is as if the Lord Himself removes the toga of the prosecutor and puts on the toga of the defense attorney. The Holy One, Blessed Be He, appropriates to Himself, so to speak, the role of the intercessor, and pleads for Israel in His very own court."[31] This self-produced intercession is displayed in a divine soliloquy imagined by the eighth-century prophet Hosea.

29. Cf. Ezekiel's variation of this idea in Ezek. 14:12-14.
30. Muffs, "Who Will Stand?" 31.
31. Muffs, "Who Will Stand?" 37.

When Israel was a child, I loved him,
    and from Egypt I called, "My son."
They [i.e., prophets such as Moses, Aaron, and Miriam][32] called
    to them,
    but they walked away from them. (Hos. 11:1-2)

In this introductory section of the oracle, Hosea traces the first two stages of the cycle, from an initial harmony between Israel and God to the people's rebellious movement away from the Deity. This is the appropriate moment, then, for repentance, for an about-face, but it is lacking.

They shall return *(shuv)* to the land of Egypt,
    and Assyria will be their king,
    because they refuse to repent *(shuv)*. . . .
My people are stuck on turning away from me.
    To the Most High they call,
    but he will not raise them. (Hos. 11:5-7)

This is the place in the cycle when the Deity is moving toward judgment and the prophet must turn to God and intercede on behalf of the people. But here, as Hosea tells the story, the turn from judgment to mercy issues from God's own interior soul-searching. Abraham stood between the Lord and the inhabitants of Sodom and Gomorrah; there was no one to intercede for two other legendary ruined towns along the Dead Sea, Adamah and Tzebo'im (Deut. 29:23), to which Hosea alludes.

How can I give you away, O Ephraim?
    [How can] I hand you over, O Israel?
How can I give you away like Adamah?
    [How can] I punish you like Tzebo'im?

32. My translation here is based on the traditional Hebrew text of Hos. 11:1, but most modern translations follow the ancient Greek version here, i.e., NRSV, "The more *I* called them, / the more they went away from *me*." I see no need to adopt the Greek version, since the Hebrew makes sense on its own terms and is parallel in meaning and form to lines attributed to another eighth-century prophet, Micah, where the role of prophetic guidance in the wake of the divine deliverance from Egypt is explicit.

> My people, what did I do to you?
>   And in what way did I weary you? Answer me.
> For I brought you up out of the land of Egypt,
>   and from the house of bondage I redeemed you.
> And I sent before you Moses, Aaron, and Miriam. (Mic. 6:3-4)

My heart turns over inside me;
    at once my compassion *(nhm)* is stoked.
I will not act [out of] my fierce anger.
    I will not turn *(shuv)* to destroy Israel,
for I am God and not a human,
    the Holy One in your midst,
    and I will not proceed in wrath.   (Hos. 11:8-9)

Here, the intercession seems to happen within the Godhead itself. At the
end of this speech, compassion overcomes anger, the first clauses of Exodus
34:6-7 ("merciful and gracious") defeat the final clauses ("punishing to the
third and fourth generations"); in Kabbalistic terms, *hesed* overpowers *din.*
The people are bent on turning away and seem incapable of turning back to
God, so God must do all the turning. When the habitual dysfunction of this
relationship reaches its rock-bottom nadir, a hidden foundation of core
identity is exposed beneath all the cult and rites, the treaties and entreaties:
the Creator desires life. As Second Isaiah will write in the wake of another
crisis (the exile) that provokes identity clarification within the Godhead,

For thus says the Lord
who created the heavens —
    yea, he is God —
who formed the earth and made it —
he did not create it to be chaos,
    he formed it to be inhabited.   (Isa. 45:18)

If, *if,* stage 4 is reached, then the divine Warrior lets it rip. The mercy
seat is empty.

Ho! I will become enraged *(nhm)* toward my foes,
    and avenge myself against my enemies.   (Isa. 1:24)

Thus says the Lord of the Heavenly Armies, . . .
The wrath of the Lord: I am full of it.
    I am weary of holding it in. . . .
I will stretch out my hand
    against the inhabitants of the land,
    saying of the Lord.   (Jer. 6:9, 11, 12)

My anger will be spent, and I will lower my fury on them. . . .
                                                       (Ezek. 5:13)

But after all the cataclysms and conflagrations, we reach stage 5, in which God cools down:

> For a trice his anger,
>   for a lifespan his blessing.   (Ps. 30:5)

Note the line that follows the ellipsis in the above verse from Ezekiel.

> My anger will be spent, and I will lower my fury on them, **and then I will calm down** *(nhm)*. (Ezek. 5:13)

And once God is becalmed *(nhm* in the Niphal), comfort *(nhm* in the Piel) emanates outward.

> You will say in that day:
> I will give thanks to you, O LORD,
>   for though you were angry with me,
> your anger turned away,
>   and you comforted *(nhm)* me.   (Isa. 12:1)

> I will turn their mourning into joy,
>   and I will comfort *(nhm)* them.   (Jer. 31:13)

The most dramatic expression of this comfort comes in the opening line of Second Isaiah. After a generation of scolding from Jeremiah and Ezekiel, this anonymous mid-sixth-century prophet whose oracles are included in the anthology of the Isaiah scroll leaves no doubt about his message. There will be no more jeremiads. The first words (in Hebrew) out of God's mouth after four decades of exile in Babylon, according to Isaiah 40:1, are

Nahamu nahamu ʿammi.

The reassuring repetition of the first two words *(nahamu nahamu)* and the kissing, nursing alliteration of the labial consonants that dominate the line *(nahamu nahamu ʿammi)* combine to form a prophetic caress. It is as if all those *mems* (the *m* of the Hebrew alphabet) in the line secretly spell out a different word, *ʾimma,* "Mommy." "Comfort, comfort my people." It is now safe to come outside. God is not angry anymore. According to the rhetoric of the prophet, we are eavesdropping on the proceedings of the divine council as God deputizes a contingent of angels to act as heralds and agents of consolation to a ravaged populace. "'Comfort, comfort my people,' says your God" (Isa. 40:1). This message is so urgent that it inverts the expected word order. The proclamation "Comfort, comfort" precedes and preempts the prophetic formula for introducing an oracle, "says your God." How beautiful upon the mountains are the feet of the messenger who brings such good news (Isa. 52:7), that God has moved through the entire emotional cycle. The narrator of the earthy narratives in Judges would describe this cosmic cease-fire with this coda, "And the land had rest." From Second Isaiah, the poet-prophet who had stood in the councils of the Lord and heard the decrees of heaven, we get loftier expression. It is time for a creation-wide carnival:

> Jubilate, O Sky, and exult, O Earth;
>> break, O Mountains, into happy jubilation.
> For the LORD has comforted *(nḥm)* his people,
>> and will have compassion on his suffering ones.   (Isa. 49:13)

Jonah: The Exception That Proves the Rule

The most common popular image of the prophet is that of the lone voice in the wilderness speaking to the community on behalf of God ("Thus says the LORD"). We often miss the other side of the coin, the image of the prophet speaking to God on behalf of the community in which he stands embedded. But both roles were part of the portfolio of biblical prophets, and the Book of the Twelve confirms this by including a narrative about an inadequate prophet in order to prove the point. Muffs writes, "The Bible does present the case of a true prophet whose prophecy is not perfect because he does not know mercy. This prophet is Jonah. . . . He is the one who asks the Lord to take his soul because death is preferable to life if divine justice is not concretized before his eyes."[33]

The Lord calls Jonah to journey to Nineveh and announce that divine judgment was imminent against the capital of the bullying superpower Assyria, a land that in Israelite eyes was an emblem of idolatry and immorality, and a cradle of sadism. The comical exploits of Jonah begin when the prophet flees (presumably from his village in central Samaria, 2 Kings 14:25) as far as he can in the opposite direction from Nineveh. Throughout the story, the piety and obedience of every phylum within creation — hu-

---

33. Muffs, "Who Will Stand?" 37.

mans such as the Phoenician sailors and the inhabitants of Nineveh, beasts of the field such as the Assyrian livestock who fast and don sackcloth, the biggest fish in the sea, the sea that storms and calms at the Lord's behest, creepers such as the worm that devours a castor bean plant that gave Jonah shade, and that plant-yielding seed itself — are contrasted with the contrariness of the prophet.

But once Leviathan's cousin vomits Jonah back onto shore, the prophet does make his way to Nineveh and delivers the message of judgment in his best imitation of his Ephraimite prophetic hero Elijah (there is a Jewish tradition that Jonah was among the disciples of Elijah):[34] "Within forty days Nineveh will be turned upside-down!" (Jon. 3:4).

But the story confounds all the stereotypes. The Ninevites repent, and their king sounds more like a Samuel than a Sennacherib when he says, "Let all persons turn *(shuv)* from their evil ways, and from the violence in their hands. Who knows? Perhaps the Deity will turn *(shuv)* and calm down *(nhm)*, and turn *(shuv)* from his fierce anger so we are not destroyed" (Jon. 3:8-9).

This is where we finally learn what bothered Jonah about this entire assignment. It was not that Jonah was reluctant to leave the comfort of home or afraid of the consequences of bearing bad news. Jonah knew that divine anger was inseparable from divine love, and the impassioned expansion of the Lord's emotional horizon to include Nineveh threatened his most cherished marker of identity, chosenness. So when the Ninevites turned from their sins and the Lord turned from the course of punishing them, "Jonah became deeply troubled and angry. And he prayed to the Lord, 'O Lord, is this not what I said when I was back on my home turf? That's why I fled toward Tarshish back in the first place, because I knew that you are a God merciful and gracious, long-nostrilled, full of mercy *(hesed)*, and relenting *(nhm)* toward doing evil'" (Jon. 4:1-2).

The Lord is essentially beneficent *and* also serious, enforcing the tough love of moral cause and effect. Morning by morning, the Lord releases the sun to run its course; evening by evening the Lord lets the moon out for its nocturnal stroll. There will be evening, there will be morning, today, and the next day, and the next, no matter the violence of the creatures.

But . . . between morning and evening there will be the day, the Day of the Lord, the Day of Judgment, the Day of Kingdom Come, the Day when

34. Louis Ginzberg, *The Legends of the Jews*, trans. H. Svold, 7 vols. (Baltimore: Johns Hopkins University Press, 1998; reprint of *The Legends of the Jews*, 7 vols. [1909-38]), 6:343.

the mountains are leveled and the valleys raised, the proud abased and the humble exalted. And the prophets had a sacred duty during the Day of the Lord when the divine anger threatened to burn hot and out of control to remind the Deity of his essential mercy. This is the true genius of the Hebrew prophets, their intercessory role, their mediating function between God and creation; the way the prophets massaged and cajoled and shamed and used every rhetorical trick they had at their disposal to move God from the light and heat of day to the benedictionary calm of God's evening, vespers-time stroll through the Garden.

We are accustomed to the prophet's address to the community, "Turn, repent." But as hard as it is to stand outside the community, alienated from the crowd, and say, "Thus says the LORD," it is even harder to stand up to God and say, "Don't judge them according to their deeds; deal with them according to your abundant mercy. After all, they are your people. You can't do that Noah thing all over again, destroying the world and starting all over again every ten generations."

This is the Jonah Principle. It is so easy to spout off, and write a letter to the editor, and see the mote, and from some elevated moral high ground and raised level of consciousness let 'em have it. But that is not a prophet. That is a bore. The true mediator must deliver the message of judgment, of moral cause and effect, of justice and righteousness, but also so deeply identify with the community that he or she would turn to God and plead their case, firmly resolved come-what-may to share their fate. Jonah wanted only half the job. The exception that proves the rule, the negative example: the collection of the Latter Prophets is completed by the inclusion of this story about a half-arsed prophet.

CHAPTER FIVE

God Needs Us

The Backstory of the Psalms

> *Through praise humans release energy that augments God's management of chaos; through lament humans report on the quality of God's management of chaos.*

The Psalms are on the itinerary of every pilgrim Bible reader. Who has not entered its gates with thanksgiving, walked its green pastures through the valley of the shadow of death, marveled at the grove of trees planted by the waters, or shed a tear by the rivers of Babylon? So many monuments, so many pilgrims, so many readers. But I do not propose to lead readers on a typical *hajj*. I want us to get off the bus and walk through the winding backstreets of this Old City to see things they never show you on the Holy Land tour. The back alley in question is a set of texts where the speaker threatens the Deity with loss of worship.

> Turn *(shuv)*, O LORD, rescue my life;
> > deliver me for the sake of your virtue *(ḥesed)*.
> For in Death, there is no mention of you.
> > In Sheol who praises you? (Ps. 6:4-5)

> What profit is in my blood
> > when I descend into the Pit?
> Can dust praise you?
> > Will it declare your truthfulness, give evidence of your reliability?
> > > (Ps. 30:9)

> For the dead, do you perform wonders?
>   Even more, do the shades rise up,
>   do they praise you?
> Is there any recital in the grave of your virtue *(ḥesed)?*
>   Your reliability in Abaddon?   (Ps. 88:10-11)

That is where we are headed, to certain rhetorically manipulative statements in the Psalms, and from there to the photosynthesis of liturgy, as blessings are mutually imparted among worshiper and worshiped. Still, some general orientation to the overall corpus is helpful before we head out on our perverse pilgrimage.

The Psalter is the centerpiece of that section of Tanakh known as "the Writings," Ketuvim. If the Torah and the Nevi'im represent divine speech directed to Moses and the prophets, respectively, then the Writings (that is, Psalms and the Wisdom literature) represent the human response, human speech directed to God.[1] What do humans have to say to God? Humans say, "Thanks, *merci, todâ, gracias, danke*." "The world works, life is a gift, we exhale in gratitude." Humans also say, "What the hell?" "The world does not work the way that the Torah promised and the prophets declared." We sigh in lament for all the broken things we know not how to repair.

But there is another aspect to both of the above. We can read the words of the psalmist who says, "Thank you," and asks, "How long?" But we cannot hear the tone of the voice. And this may be the key to understanding the drama of the psalms. Jon Levenson has attempted to describe the sand that produces the hermeneutic pearl of great price hidden in the ordered, versified psalters we read. It is the "painful and yawning gap between the liturgical affirmation of God's absolute sovereignty and the empirical reality of evil triumphant and unchecked."[2]

You stand in that "painful and yawning gap" when you say either "Thanks" or "What the hell?" Let us pretend that we are in the dialogic of the African American preaching event, with call and response. The Torah and the Nevi'im are the call from the preacher, the Ketuvim in general and the Psalter in particular are the response of the congregation, and we are left waiting for the next move in the sequence. For no shouts from the amen corner are innocent; they affirm, they beckon, occasionally they

---

1. Walter Brueggemann, *The Creative Word: Canon as a Model for Biblical Education* (Philadelphia: Fortress, 1982), 93.

2. Jon D. Levenson, *Creation and the Persistence of Evil: The Jewish Drama of Divine Omnipotence* (San Francisco: Harper and Row, 1988), 19.

protest, always they shape the very discourse of the preacher. In a similar way, the psalms seek to move God.

There is a story in the Psalms. The five books of the Psalter and the 150 psalms in the Masoretic tradition have an uneven distribution of laments and petitions, on the one hand, and thanksgivings and praise songs, on the other hand. As James Crenshaw has observed, laments dominate book 1 of the Psalter (Pss. 1–41), while praise songs dominate books 4 and 5 (Pss. 90–150).[3] If we can generalize, the psalms near the beginning of the scroll are characterized by petition, and the psalms near the end by praise. The Psalter tells the story, not of any life, but of a particular life, a life in tune with the peculiar contradictions of life with God. In this regard, Crenshaw describes a journey from "grief to thanksgiving, from lament to praise."[4] We can imagine, then, the Psalter sketching the course of such a life, moving from need to mature affirmation, moving from "Why? Why? Why?" to "It just is. It just is. It just is." It is a life dominated by petition early, by request, by neediness. But the Psalter ends in the same way that we hope and pray our lives will end, in delight and praise, in, as Walter Brueggemann says, an affirmation, a "yes" to God, "that goes beyond thanks for services rendered."[5]

The Psalter ends in a crescendo of such praise. Consider the final psalm:

> Praise the LORD *(hallelu Yah)!*
> Praise God in his sanctuary;
>   praise him in his august skydome.
> Praise him for his heroics;
>   praise him for the multitude of his bounty.
> Praise him with blasts from the shofar;
>   praise him with the twelve-string lyre and the seven-string lyre.
> Praise him with drum and reel;
>   praise him with strings and flute.
> Praise him with loud cymbals;
>   praise him with ringing cymbals.
> Let all that breathes praise the LORD *(hallelu Yah)!*
> Praise the LORD *(hallelu Yah)!* (Ps. 150:1-6)

---

3. James L. Crenshaw, *The Psalms: An Introduction* (Grand Rapids: Eerdmans, 2001), 3.

4. Crenshaw, *The Psalms*, 3.

5. Walter Brueggemann, *Theology of the Old Testament: Testimony, Dispute, Advocacy* (Minneapolis: Fortress, 1997), 476.

There is something in this crescendo of praise that, at first glance, is false, hyped, over the top, overcompensating. But its sounding brass and clanging cymbals are not merely hollow musical dramatics. Because you cannot simply turn to the final psalms of praise; before you get to them you must live through the hundred-plus that precede the final jubilations. You receive the prize of praise only after all the petition and pain of the previous psalms. The praise of Psalm 150 is the delight and joy of those acquainted with grief, an autumnal, reflective, bittersweet joy and praise, a sober, clear-eyed, anything-but-naive "Yes" to the entire mess. That is the human story in the Psalms.

There is another story in the Psalter. It consists of the story of two partners in a complicated relationship. The Psalter knows them as Israel and the Lord; we might also speak of humanity and God, or created and Creator. Consider the words of Psalm 5:4 with a slight emendation that gets to what I am talking about, the edgy desperation, the tentativeness, the unspoken questioning behind all the courtly flattery before the throne of the King of the Universe.

You are not a God who delights in wickedness, *are you?*
Evil will not sojourn with you, *will it?*

In this drama, humans are the prompters, reminding God of what is written in the script.

So the theology of the Psalms has a lot of psychology mixed up in it. The Psalter represents the worship manual of the priests of the First and Second Temples in Jerusalem. They imagined that the inner sanctum of that temple represented the throne room of the Creator of the Universe, the King, the Sovereign. Before God's throne, then, these supplicants petitioned, begged for mercy, and, perhaps most importantly, gave God status reports on what was happening outside the temple gates. "Wake up," "Arise," "Be as good as Moses said you were in Exodus 34:6-7." The priests had to move God, to cajole and flatter God, to remind God of what God had promised the community and humanity and the natural order: consistency, justice, harmony, regularity, cause and effect.

The petitions and laments of the psalms are indirect evidence of human dependence upon God. We need God. But what does the crescendo of praise and of thanksgiving suggest? Does God need our praise? We saw already several psalms in which the worshiper extorts God with the threat of loss of praise. "If I die, who will praise you?" "If I, at Sheol's door, fall through to the other side, won't you feel the loss?" The psychology of these pleas seems to be, "Hey, God, you need me too." It is as if Psalm 22:3 is actually true: "The LORD *is enthroned* on the praises of Israel." Without their praises, God's sovereignty is diminished, imperiled, unrealized. Without their praises, the biblical God might be reduced to the ranks of those other forlorn personages in that cave where all the gods of dead cults must retire, where all those former big shots sourly hibernate, attracting no awe, receiving no cult, powerless to influence the worlds they brought into being.

Food for the Gods

The idea that God needs our praise and worship parallels an old idea in religion, one that is explicit in the religion of ancient Israel's neighboring cultures and implicit in certain biblical texts, namely, that the gods require the ministrations of their servants in order to perform their royal functions. Gods require praise just like they require food. The temples of Egypt, Canaan, Turkey, Syria, and Iraq were imagined to be divine palaces; priests served as the domestics — butlers, maids, cooks, and cleaners — in these precincts; and the morning and evening sacrifices were meals prepared for the gods' consumption.

As the biblical scholar Karel van der Toorn writes,

> The actual cult in ancient Syro-Palestine consisted primarily of "the care and feeding of the gods," to use a phrase coined by A. Leo Oppenheim for the Mesopotamian temple ritual. Apart from the administration of the temple and its estate, the tasks of the priests involved the preparation and presentation of the daily meals to the god, the toilette of the deity, and such domestic chores as cleaning. The regular offerings were brought in twice a day, once in the morning and once at evening, in analogy with the two meals a day that were customary in the Mediterranean world.[6]

In several places the Bible explicitly denies that sacrifices, animal or vegetable, provide the Lord with nourishment.

---

6. Karel van der Toorn, "Theology, Priests, and Worship in Canaan and Ancient Israel," in *Civilizations of the Ancient Near East*, III-IV, ed. Jack Sasson (Peabody, Mass.: Hendrickson, 2000), 2053.

"I will not accept from your house a steer,
    from your fields, goats.
For all the beasts of the forest are mine,
    the cattle on a thousand hills.
I know every bird of the mountains,
    every cricket of the field is with me.
If I were hungry, I would not tell you,
    for the world and all that fills it is mine.
Do I eat the meat of bulls?
    And the blood of goats do I drink?"   (Ps. 50:9-13)

I will celebrate the name of God with a song,
    and I will magnify him with a thanksgiving.
And this will be more pleasant to the LORD than an ox,
    a steer with a horn and hoofs.   (Ps. 69:30-31)

And there is the prophet Micah's classic expression of this theme:

With what shall I present myself before the LORD,
    and prostrate before the Most High?
Shall I present myself with burnt offerings,
    with calves a year old?
Will the LORD be favorable to thousands of rams,
    with ten thousand rivers of olive oil?   (Mic. 6:6-7)

So what does the God of Israel seek from his servants, if not the food of slaughtered fauna and processed flora?

He has declared to you, O humanity, what is pleasing;
    and what does the LORD seek from you?
This: perform justice *(mishpaṭ),*
    and love loyalty *(ḥesed),*
    and with the utmost care walk with your God.   (Mic. 6:8)

Yet, as the biblical scholar Gary Anderson points out, many other biblical passages could be read as suggesting the opposite view, that sacrifice does function as sustenance for the Lord. "To be sure, [Psalm 50] explicitly says that YHWH needs no food. But before quickly concluding that the Bible's account of sacrifice is on a higher evolutionary level [than the texts from Israel's neighboring cultures that depict sacrifice as food for the gods], one must account for the enormous amount of evidence that portrays Israelite sacrifice as food for YHWH. Countless texts from every period describe YHWH's sacrifices as food."[7] As evidence Anderson lists biblical references to the altar as "the LORD's table" (e.g., Mal. 1:7, 12; cf. Exod. 25:23-30; Lev. 24:6; 1 Kings 7:48; Ezek. 40:39-43), to sacrifices as God's "food" (e.g., Lev. 3:11; 21:6; Num. 28:2; Ezek. 44:7), and to "the aroma of the burnt offerings [as] 'a sweet savor' to the LORD" (e.g., Lev. 3:16; Num. 28:24; cf. Gen. 8:21).[8] The best we can say is that there are places where the Bible describes sacrifice as food for the Deity and places where it critiques this very idea, a debate that, Anderson points out, was going on at the same time in the cultures of Israel's neighbors as witnessed in late revisions to the Babylonian account of the primeval flood that delete references to the gods dining on human food.[9] In a single psalm, the efficacy of sacrifice could be critiqued and affirmed.

> My lord, open my lips,
> and my mouth will declare your praise song.
> For you do not desire sacrifice,
> and if I give burnt offerings you will not be pleased.
> The sacrifice to God is a broken spirit;
> a heart broken and crushed, O God, you will not despise.
>
> (Ps. 51:15-17)

The poet here stands with the prophets and their critique of ritual performance untethered from "walking humbly with your God." But that is not the end of the matter. Once the proud have turned from their sins, their sacrifices, formerly scorned, are celebrated.

> Do good in your pleasure to Zion;
> rebuild the walls of Jerusalem.
> Then you will delight in righteous sacrifices,
> burnt offerings and whole offerings;
> then bulls will be burned on your altar. (Ps. 51:18-19)

It is commonplace for sympathetic biblical interpreters to soft-pedal the evidence for sacrifice as food for the Lord. After all, such a view reeks

---

7. Gary A. Anderson, "Sacrifice and Sacrificial Offerings (OT)," in *Anchor Bible Dictionary*, ed. D. N. Freedman, 6 vols. (New York: Doubleday, 1992), 5:872.

8. Anderson, "Sacrifice and Sacrificial Offerings," 872.

9. Gary A. Anderson, *Sacrifices and Offerings in Ancient Israel: Studies in Their Social and Political Importance*, Harvard Semitic Monographs 41 (Atlanta: Scholars, 1987), 16-19.

of a form of magical thinking unworthy of prophetic religion. The remarks of the biblical scholar Patrick Miller are typical. Miller acknowledges that "remnants of this notion of sacrifice as food for the deity persisted in ancient Israelite religion . . . in fairly muted form," but that, on the whole, "Israelite sacrificial practice moved in another direction."[10] To be sure, the sacrificial system — the presentation of meat and grain offerings upon a sacred table in the Jerusalem temple, God's house — served a variety of functions and cannot be reduced to a single notion. Sacrifices served social purposes, Miller notes, such as providing food for the priesthood and the poor.[11] Sacrifices were a form of communication through ritual, Anderson notes, that vividly diagrammed the syntax of the relationship between God and Israel: God as primary subject and ultimate donor, Israel as grateful recipient, then subsequent donor.[12]

C. S. Lewis, the eloquent modern apologist for orthodox Christianity, addressed this problem from another angle. Though Lewis did not discuss the notion of sacrifice as food for the gods, he did examine the rhetorical bargaining in the Psalms that ultimately stems from that idea. "As for the element of bargaining in the Psalms (do this and I will praise you), that silly dash of paganism surely existed. The flame does not ascend pure from the altar. But the impurities are not its essence."[13] Lewis deftly lampoons the image of a vain God who demands courtly praise and flattery and explains, to the contrary, that the sacrifices of praise demanded of worshipers in the Psalms represent gestures that provide us with access to God: "[I]t is in the process of being worshipped that God communicates his presence to men"; "praise not merely expresses [the relationship between God and humanity] but completes the enjoyment," implying that as in love, intimacy is deepened when acts of bonding are mingled with verbal praise, with the pillow talk of liturgy.[14]

But what is so primitive or pagan about the idea that reality is interactive, that there is something within us that belongs to God? With the destruction of the Second Temple, animal and cereal offerings came to an end in Judaism and daily prayers replaced daily sacrifices. The backstory

10. Patrick D. Miller, *The Religion of Ancient Israel*, Library of Ancient Israel (Louisville: Westminster John Knox, 2000), 126-27.

11. Miller, *Religion of Ancient Israel*, 121-22.

12. Gary A. Anderson, "Israelite Religion," in *The New Interpreter's Bible* 1, ed. Leander Keck (Nashville: Abingdon, 1994), 279-80.

13. C. S. Lewis, *Reflections on the Psalms* (New York: Harcourt and Brace, 1958), 97.

14. Lewis, *Reflections on the Psalms*, 93, 95.

of sacrifice as food for the gods is transformed into a more dynamic and abstract but no less vital transaction: God *is hungry,* for relationship, and this is verbalized through praise song and lament.

A Sacrifice of Praise

The evolution from offerings of sacrifice to offerings of praise is already present in the Psalter, before the destruction of the temple in 70 C.E. The dynamic, however, is no different. The speaker in the Psalms understands that he, that she, possesses something God needs. Hence, the bargaining ("do this and I will praise you") to which C. S. Lewis referred.

> Be merciful to me, O LORD;
>> see my suffering caused by my haters,
>> O one who raises up from the gates of Death;
>> so that I might recite all your praise songs
>> in the gates of Daughter Zion,
>> [and] jubilate in your deliverance.   (Ps. 9:13-14)

God will lose something too, these texts brashly declare, if the pitiable speaker is not rescued. The Holy One is, as Psalm 22:3 says, "enthroned on the praise songs of Israel," and on this basis the speaker in this psalm pleads for help in a later stanza.

> Rescue my life . . . from the sword;
>> deliver me from the mouth of the lion.   (Ps. 22:20)

Then (it is implied),

> I will recite your name to my brothers;
>> in the midst of the congregation I will celebrate you.   (Ps. 22:22)

The transactional dynamic — if you rescue me, then I will praise you — is too common to be a mere "pagan" remnant. It appears in many psalms.

> Rescue us, O LORD, our God,
>> and gather us from the nations
> to praise your holy name,
>> to do worship with your praise songs.   (Ps. 106:47)

Help us, my God, rescue us
　　for the sake of the glory of your name. . . .
And we your people, the flock of your pasture,
　　will praise you forever.
From generation to generation, we will recite your praise songs.

　　　　　　　　　　　　　　　　　　　　　　　　　(Ps. 79:9, 13)

Bring my life out of prison
　　so that I might praise your name.　　　　　　　　　(Ps. 142:7)

Hear, O God, my cry.
　　Draw near to my prayer. . . .
Then I will rhapsodize your name forever.　　　　　　　(Ps. 61:1, 8)

Jon Levenson has traced through the Hebrew Bible the themes of the fragility of creation, the *Perils of Pauline*-like "drama" of divine sovereignty, and God's drafting of Israel to serve as partner in the *shalom* project. Against the background of Levenson's analysis, the above sentiments of the psalmist are fitting expressions of the mutuality of covenant. Levenson writes: "[T]he [divine-human] relationship includes the possibility that YHWH's congregation might activate their lord's dormant mastery through their cultic action and thus actualize those nearly discredited creative wonders."[15] Those cultic actions include lament and praise. "YHWH's kingship in Israel, like . . . his mastery over creation, remained vulnerable and in continual need of reaffirmation, reratification, reacclamation. The covenant of Sinai has not the fixity and irrevocability of a royal decree; demanding human participation, it is fully realized only with the glad consent of the cultic community of Israel."[16]

To summarize, among the relics in the cellar of the cathedral of the Psalms is an old idea, of sacrifice as food for the gods. Such a notion is a vivid, rawly anthropomorphic encapsulation of a truth that was true in the beginning, is now, and ever shall be, that God does need worship from us. Aboveground, in the central chamber of the Psalter, the medium for this exchange is debated, nuanced, and ultimately transformed from that of the food chain to the praise song. But the physics of liturgical photosynthesis are still in force. Praise releases something inside us that belongs to God. Surely, this is what is implied in the frequent command in the Psalter and

15. Levenson, *Creation*, 26.
16. Levenson, *Creation*, 138.

Bible for worshipers "to bless the LORD." Humans possess some measure of love-energy drawn from, in Kabbalistic terms, the gracious endowment created in the world-making big bang of the primeval *tzimtzum*, that contraction of the Infinite that gave space for the plentitude of finites. When we "bless" the Lord, we release our vital powers back to their source, an act of restoration that contributes to the mending, *tikkun*, of creation.

Sweet Psalmist of Israel

At the beginning of this chapter, we enumerated two stories in the Psalter: the way the very structure of the Psalter as a whole traces the contours of a full human life from petition to praise, and the way the poetry of the Psalter penetrates deeper than the narrative sections of Scripture to reveal the emotions and dynamics of the covenant relationship between the Lord and Israel. There is one more story in the Psalter. It is the story of David.

David is associated with the book of Psalms in two ways. First, the Hebrew phrase *le-David* binds David to almost half of the psalms (to 71 out of 150). It is not clear what this prepositional phrase inserted by scribes means; *le-* can mean "by" as in "[written] by David," or "for" as in "[dedicated] for David," or "belonging to" as in "[belonging] to David" or "[belonging] to [the] David[ic collection of psalms]." Second, in 13 psalms in the Hebrew Bible (the Greek Bible, the Septuagint, contains 16), the psalm is prefaced with sentences that explicitly link it with a specific event in David's story. For instance, Psalm 51 bears this superscription: "A Psalm of David, when the prophet Nathan came to him, after he had gone into Bathsheba," so that readers imagine this remorse-filled confession as David's petition for forgiveness and emotional resurrection after Nathan's rebuke. No longer high and mighty, David sees himself for who he is, adulterer, abuser, conspirator, and murderer; a traitor to every woman who loved him and every man who served him (cf. 2 Sam. 12:1-15). Through the tradition that David authored many psalms, and through these early examples of midrash by which scribes linked the prose of 1–2 Samuel with the poetry of the Psalms, the Psalter has become David's book and David's story.

What is so special about David? David shares traits with many of the other heroes from the frontier period of biblical history. He is braggart, pretender, madman, ambusher, blood-feuder, murderer, conspirator, bushwhacker, assassin, giant-slayer, lion-killer, mutilator, outlaw, wife-stealer, and more. David stands above, just barely, this larger group — Samson, Saul, Joab, and so many more heroes and antiheroes from Judges and Samuel — in his ability to plan, to express magnanimity, to at times see beyond clannish blood-vengeance to a new community. What was his secret? What set David apart?

Although the ascription of Davidic authorship to so many psalms must be seen in light of the ancient penchant for associating biblical scrolls with great figures from the past (the Pentateuch with Moses, the Wisdom literature with Solomon), the traditions about David, "the sweet singer of Israel" (2 Sam. 23:1), have the ring of authenticity. Thus in the biblical tradition, David is both hero and bard. He is both combatant in the arena and its observer. For instance, according to the tradition of 2 Samuel 1, he has the perspective to compose the funeral speech for a fallen rival. Whether indicative of a firm grasp of Realpolitik, an artistic perspective, or creaturely sympathy, this ability to humanize an enemy is remarkable and, whether in the story world or the historical world, is suggestive of David's rare greatness.

Let us consider an ancient definition of heroism, from Andrew George's translation of *The Epic of Gilgamesh*. In its opening lines, the protagonist of world literature's first great quest to be written down and have survived, the grandfather of Odysseus, Ulysses, and Sinbad, is described as follows:

> He came a far road, was weary, found peace,
> and set all his labours on a tablet of stone.[17]

The greatest hero lives to tell the tale, yea, lives *and* tells the tale. Similarly, David was both participant and observer, actor and artist; like the great English soldier-poets of World War 1, like the great American soldier-novelists of World War 2.

To live fully, to sin boldly, to watch children self-destruct before your eyes: what an irresistible mass of contradictions David was. The music, the violence; the cunning, the mercy: the highs and lows of David. And, most of all, this: to be the apple of YHWH's eye.

Why did God favor David? What was his magic? His charm against the divine anger? His mediation? Abraham negotiated. Moses talked back. What did David do? David sang, David strummed, David danced. Did

---

17. Andrew George, *The Epic of Gilgamesh: A New Translation* (New York: Barnes and Noble, 1999), 1.

these performances bring a kind of grace? an absolution? a mediation? Did David's music have the same effect on God that it did on Saul? "And whenever an [evil] spirit of God came upon Saul, David took the lyre and played it with his hand, and a [good] spirit came upon Saul, and he felt better, and the evil spirit departed from him" (1 Sam. 16:23).

The Davidic backstory of the Psalter, finally, yields a backstory behind it. Just as the musician David was able to calm Saul's spells of madness with his lyre-playing, the exhalations of every free soul's measure of vitality, offered for Love, offered to Love, perform an essential service. Praise releases the love-energy inside us that belongs to God. That is the backstory of the Psalms.

CHAPTER SIX

The Blueprint

The Backstory of Wisdom

Here and there, humans catch glimpses of the divine design for chaos management; living according to these insights is another expression of the partnership.

The biblical books of Proverbs, Job, and Ecclesiastes are referred to as "Wisdom literature." That is not what the Bible calls them; it is what we call them because of what they share in common with each other and with literary collections from other cultures that contain proverbs, practical instructions, and essays about the meaning of life. There is Wisdom literature in other parts of Scripture because "wisdom" is not simply a type of literature; it is a sphere of life.

Parents dispense wisdom to children through instruction, lectures, and sayings ("From your mouth to God's ear"). Elders in traditional cultures — whether the men who gathered around the city gate or certain wise women known for their discernment — crack wise, riddle, argue, quell hot heads, settle disputes, and dispense advice in pithy, memorable ways with a vast assortment of proverbs that they take pride in selecting and using at *just* the right time. In the side chambers of ancient palaces, when the scribes were not taking royal dictation, copying or recopying scrolls and tablets in archives, cataloguing the items in the royal treasury, or translating diplomatic correspondence from and into foreign languages, they wrote arty, urban proverbs and essays about wisdom themes. These ancient intellectuals also wrote liturgical poems in homage to their matron, Ḥokma, Lady Wisdom. The Wisdom literature originated from the popular proverbs that were the currency of everyday speech emanating from family and village, from parents and elders; and from a scribal culture, the intelligentsia, who composed sentences, paragraphs, essays, dialogues, and other literary products with wisdom themes.

The Wisdom literature stands out in the Bible because it contains few references to the specific history of Israel. In Job, Proverbs, and Ecclesiastes, you do not hear references to the exodus or the covenant, to Moses or David or the temple. Wisdom literature is based not on the events of Israelite history, but on the events of prehistory, on creation. This has several implications. Wisdom literature is the most international of biblical genres: there are countless examples of biblical proverbs or wisdom sayings that have close parallels with Egyptian or Canaanite or Mesopotamian wisdom. This is extraordinary. While so much of the Bible is about being different, Wisdom literature highlights truth that Israel held in common with other cultures. Also, Wisdom literature does not often use Israel's special name for the Deity, YHWH. Proverbs does, but Ecclesiastes does not at all, not even once. And in the main section of Job, the dialogues of Job 3–37, the word "YHWH" occurs only a single time.

For some, these latter books, Ecclesiastes and Job especially, are bewildering, more statements of doubt than of faith, and the way they do not highlight the special themes, the salvation history, makes them dangerous. They are about the God of creation, before God got local with Abraham, before God revealed the sacred name to Moses. For some, however, these very books can be the gateway into the Bible, into community, into faith, because in Ecclesiastes and Job universal themes of existence are engaged, and the questions raised in these books in particular serve as antidotes to the poisonously parochial pieties of many other parts of Scripture.

The Blueprint

As the Roman Catholic biblical scholar Richard Clifford has written, biblical Wisdom literature teaches that there is a cosmic order.[1] It is an article of faith in the wisdom tradition that behind the manifold and particular incidents and accidents of apparent unmeaning there is a matrix. In Egypt,

---

1. Richard J. Clifford, "Introduction to Wisdom Literature," in *The New Interpreter's Bible*, ed. Leander Keck (Nashville: Abingdon, 1997), 5:9.

this order was personified as a goddess, Ma'at; in the book of Proverbs, this cosmic order is also personified as female; she is *hokma*, "Wisdom." My professor James Kugel had another term for this cosmic order: "the Great Plan."

This cosmic order can go by many names. In the Hebrew Bible, the Great Plan can be referred to by the word *hokma* itself, or by *'esa*, the "design."

> O LORD, you are my God;
>   I will exalt you, I will praise your name.
> For you have done wonders,
>   a design *('esa)* from of old, secure and true.   (Isa. 25:1)

> For I am God, and there is no other;
>   [I am] God and there is none like me,
> declaring from beginning to end,
>   and from olden days before anything was made,
> the one who says, "My design *('esa)* will stand
>   and all my intentions I will make happen."   (Isa. 46:9-10)

I can now see that this concept is akin to what in my childhood Baptist church we referred to as "the will of God." A sentence such as Isaiah 5:19, "May the design *('esa)* of the Holy One of Israel hasten to occur," is another way of saying "Thy will be done."

In an essay on Job 28, the Jewish biblical scholar Kugel compares the Great Plan (and the Hebrew *'esa*, "design," is especially apt in this analogy) to an immense sheet of graph paper containing the universal blueprint. "The great divine plan that underlies all reality is like a detailed design drawn on graph paper. Since the graph paper is basically hidden, no one can ever hope to survey its entirety. But here and there, individual sages have caught a glimpse of one little part of it, one little square on the graph paper, and if we can preserve their insights one by one and eventually put them together, then we will nonetheless have something, some individual parts of the divine plan. Perhaps we may even get some feeling for what the whole plan is like."[2] This order, this *hokma*, this Great Plan, according to wisdom teaching, as seen in Proverbs 8:22-31 or Job 28, was sewn into the fabric of reality "in the beginning," during creation week. Proverbs 8 be-

---

2. James Kugel, *The Great Poems of the Bible: A Reader's Companion with New Translations* (New York: Free Press, 1999), 112.

gins, "Does not *hokma* [Wisdom] call and *tebunah* [Understanding] offer her voice?" That rhetorical question introduces her speech. Then she has this to say about herself.

> The LORD produced me [i.e., Wisdom] in the beginning of his
>   activities,
>   prior to his works of olden days.   (Prov. 8:22)

In this Song of Herself, Wisdom recalls her partnership with God that began at daybreak, day one:

> Ages ago, I was shaped,
>   from the start of the primeval times of the earth.   (Prov. 8:23)

The poet in Proverbs 8:24-29 walks us through all those evenings and mornings. "When there were not any depths," "when there were no springs," "before mountains," "before hills," "when [God] had not yet made earth," "when [God] erected heaven"; the guided tour through creation week continues with Wisdom — surveyor, architect, engineer, mason, creatrix; above all, a boon companion — step-by-step, in step with God.

> I was right beside him, an adviser;
> I was a delight, daily,
>   laughing before him at every instant.   (Prov. 8:30)

In this exuberant retelling of Genesis 1 in Proverbs 8, we find the explanation for why everything the Lord God made was so "very good." The pleasure dome emanated from Elohim's joyful, playful collaboration with Wisdom.

In another biblical poem, in Job 28, Wisdom is less a personal partner of the Creator as in Proverbs 8, and more like physics itself, that underlying cosmic system of grammar that allows for the translation of divine utterance, "let there be," into the meaningful form "and there was."

> When he made the wind of [a certain] weight,
>   and calculated for water its measurements;
> when he made laws for the rain,
>   and a path for the sound-blast [i.e., thunder];
> then: he saw her [i.e., Wisdom, *hokma*], and he declared her;
>   he framed her, yea, he [fully] examined her.   (Job 28:25-27)

With various degrees of personification, these texts testify to the ancient sages' faith in the existence of a Great Plan. According to Kugel's analogy, each square on the blueprint contains a single truth about how life works. Humans, according to Kugel's reading of the biblical Wisdom literature, are capable of discovering these small truths. Two plus two makes four. What goes up, must come down. "Pride goeth before . . . a fall" (Prov. 16:18 KJV). "Like mother, like daughter" (Ezek. 16:44). But each of the major wisdom books in the Bible — Proverbs, Ecclesiastes, and Job — deals with the blueprint in a different way. All these works affirm the existence of a cosmic order, of a Great Plan, but the next teaching of Wisdom literature was open for question. Are humans capable of seeing the blueprint? Can the great code be deciphered?

The book of Proverbs is optimistic. Humans are capable of observing details in the blueprint accurately. The book of Ecclesiastes is pessimistic: there is a Great Plan, but a mist of vanity (Hebrew *hebel*) obscures our ability to see it. The book of Job tells an adventure story about a man propelled against his will on a quest who, for an instant and no longer than that, glimpsed the Great Plan, and saw that it contained something that the composers of Proverbs and Ecclesiastes never imagined, a square for "chaos." Let us look more closely at how each of these books builds off this backstory.

The Blueprint in Proverbs

On their good days (and they were feeling flush when they wrote the book of Proverbs) the sages taught that if one began with an awareness of God, the fear of God, one could, over time, see some of the patterns on the blueprint. But you needed to slow down, keep your mouth shut and your eyes open, mind your manners, control your temper, take the long view, and above all, be patient; then you might see some of the plan.[3] After all, it is built into creation. Why, look at the way fools behave; look at the way wise folks behave.

> The heart of the righteous muses before answering;
> the mouth of the wicked spouts trouble.   (Prov. 15:28)

> The bread of dishonesty is sweet to a man,
> but later it fills his mouth with gravel-stone.   (Prov. 20:17)

---

3. Kugel, *Great Poems*, 123.

Why, look at the ways animals behave.

> There are four small things on the earth,
>   and they are the wisest of the wise.
> The ants: a nation without might,
>   and yet they supply their food in the dry season;
> badgers: a nation without strength,
>   and yet they establish their homes in crags.
> There is no king among locusts,
>   yet they manage to march out together in ranks.
> A lizard, you can hold in your hand,
>   and yet, there it is, in the palaces of kings.   (Prov. 30:24-28)

The sages proved their "it-happens-every-day," "they'll-do-it-every-time" case by drawing from a treasury of self-evident maxims. Each of these terse parallel sayings fits snugly, employing Kugel's analogy, into a single small square on the graph paper of the blueprint. We might call this type of religious insight "natural theology," an understanding of God based on experience and observation; it is revealed, but in the sense of being uncovered here below on earth, not bursting through from heaven above. The eighteenth-century English poet William Blake understood it:

> To see a World in a Grain of Sand
> And a Heaven in a Wild Flower
> Hold Infinity in the palm of your hand
> And Eternity in an hour.[4]

Wisdom, with God's grace, can be gained through observation; it also helps to be older because only the mature have had time to get a feeling for the pattern. The supreme virtue of the wise is patience, the patience that allows one to keep believing in and living by the Great Plan despite the tragic elements of life.[5]

Creation theology is the foundation of biblical wisdom. God created a world that works. Reality has a Creator. There is a Great Plan. The universe is not a carnival Upside Down House. Here gravity prevails and grace prevails. Creation theology affirms that, in the words of the King James Ver-

---

4. William Blake, "Auguries of Innocence," ll. 1-4, in *The Complete Poetry and Prose of William Blake*, ed. David V. Eerdman (Berkeley: University of California Press, 1982), 490.

5. Kugel, *Great Poems*, 123.

sion, charity never faileth. There is a groove that God carved out during creation week that we might call the path of righteousness. To some extent people can observe its course, and the various maxims of Proverbs mark its boundaries. The book of Proverbs asks us to patiently bear all things, believe all things, hope all things, so that we might endure all things. If you enter this path of righteousness and stay on course, the sages declared, you will prosper because you are in fundamental harmony with the essential trajectories of creation.

One of Job's know-it-all comforters, Eliphaz, speaks for this wisdom tradition on its good days.

> "I would seek God,
>   and God-ward I would set my course."   (Job 5:8)

For if a person does this, as Eliphaz assures Job,

> "You will be in covenant with the field stones,
>   and the wild creatures of the field will make peace with you. . . .
> You will arrive at the grave as ripe
>   as the stands of grain arrive at the threshing floor."   (Job 5:23, 26)

The Blueprint in Ecclesiastes

The writer of the book of Ecclesiastes also affirms the existence of a pattern. There is a Great Plan.

> For everything there is a season,
> and a time for every experience under heaven.
> There is a time of birth and a time of death,
> a time of seeding and a time of weeding,
> a time of killing and a time of healing,
> a time of breaking and a time of building,
> a time of weeping and a time of playfulness,
> a time of lament and a time of leaping,
> a time of stone-scattering and a time of stone-gathering,
> a time of embracing and a time distant from embracing,
> a time of searching and a time of losing,
> a time of keeping and a time of throwing away,
> a time of ripping and a time of seaming,

a time of silence and a time of speech,
a time of love and a time of hate,
a time of war and a time of peace.   (Eccles. 3:1-8)

The polarities sketched in this justly celebrated poem span the entire orbit of our lives, of every season. The intuitions of Pete Seeger, who transformed this text into the popular folk song "Turn, Turn, Turn," were correct. This poem is about turnings, the cycles and circles and patterns and progressions that govern existence. The correct sense of the Hebrew is not, however, that "there is a time *to* be born and a time *to* die," as if we get to choose. Rather, the wisdom of this text is that there is — like it or not; for better, for worse — a time *when* folks get born and a time *when* folks die.

But there is an ethic implicit in this poem. There are choices for us to make. Given the varied seasons and times, those with ears to hear would be wise to moderate their behavior accordingly. When you find yourself stuck in a moment when things break, neither lose hope nor make it worse through quixotic struggle: let go. Do not fight the difficult times; find the breathing exercises that make the contractions bearable. When you find yourself in a time of playfulness, do not resist it but seize it: make hay, make whoopee, while the sun is shining.

Here in poetic form is the blueprint with lots of its squares filled in. There is no stronger affirmation in Scripture of the Great Plan than here in Ecclesiastes 3. But most interpreters, including Pete Seeger and the Protestant guide to Bible reading in Sunday services (that is, the Revised Common Lectionary), stop reading too soon and miss the punch line that follows this inspired piece of Serenity-Prayer insight. "The entire thing [God] has made beautiful according to its time. Furthermore, [God] has given the [ability to comprehend] chronology in their hearts. Yet: humans cannot discover what God is enacting from beginning to end" (Eccles. 3:11). The squares are there, but we lack the perspective to see the patterns they form. Humans lack the perspective to see the larger patterns that the squares are forming. We can control this small truth, and this one, filling in random squares here and there, but never be able to see the design, the shape, of the entire thing. When we are in the middle of a situation, we do not know if it is a time when something is being born or something is dying.

But an even more fundamental problem lies at the heart of the wisdom of Ecclesiastes: the Great Plan is shrouded by a mist of *hebel*, the Hebrew word that Saint Jerome around 400 C.E. translated into Latin as *vanitas*. "Vanity of vanities, saith the Preacher, vanity of vanities, all is vanity"

(Eccles. 1:2 KJV). That is the formulation with which English readers are most familiar, but it is not entirely accurate. The Hebrew word *hebel* has something to do with the wind, and with its visible aspects; those manifestations of wind that can be seen: "mist," "steam," "puff [of smoke]," "vapor."[6] The biblical scholar R. B. Y. Scott, accordingly, eschews the shopworn "vanity" in his translation of Ecclesiastes 1:2.

> Breath of a breath! (says Qoheleth). The slightest breath!
> All is a breath.[7]

James Kugel's translation of this refrain found throughout Ecclesiastes also gets at this. "So fleeting, said Koheleth, everything is so fleeting."[8]

"Mist of mists," "vapor of vapors": these are better representations of Qoheleth's (the Hebrew name of the book) thinking than "vanity of vanities" because we associate "vanity" with emptiness and falsity and nullity. But the biblical sage who here assumed the voice of Solomon, a man who "had seen it all, knew it all, and had it all," is not saying that everything is without form and void of meaning.[9] Rather, there is meaning and substance, to everything there is a season and a time, but we see through a glass darkly. A man who wrote the book (one of the finest of them, at any rate) on Hebrew linguistics and another on Ecclesiastes, Choon-Leong Seow, says the following about what *hebel* signifies in Qoheleth's argument.[10] Through his use of *hebel*, Qoheleth "does not mean that everything is meaningless or insignificant, but that everything is beyond human apprehension and comprehension."[11] Our apprehension of the code — of *ḥokma*, of the *ʿeṣa*, of the Great Plan — is ephemeral and elusive. We have intimations of immortalities, but no more than that, and the second we imagine that we have grasped the truth — poof! — it is gone. We can experience these exuberances, fleeting puffs of insight about and engagement with the Real, but we can neither possess nor control them.

---

6. K. Seybold, *"hebhel,"* in *Theological Dictionary of the Old Testament*, vol. 3 (Grand Rapids: Eerdmans, 1978), 315; Choon-Leong Seow, *Ecclesiastes*, Anchor Bible 18C (New York: Doubleday, 1997), 47.

7. R. B. Y. Scott, *Proverbs, Ecclesiastes*, Anchor Bible 18 (Garden City, N.Y.: Doubleday, 1965), 209.

8. Kugel, *Great Poems*, 306.

9. Cf. Seow (*Ecclesiastes*, 48) for this characterization of Solomon.

10. I am referring to Seow, *Ecclesiastes* (1997) and *A Grammar for Biblical Hebrew* (Nashville: Abingdon, 1987).

11. Seow, *Ecclesiastes*, 59.

This is Qoheleth's brilliantly ambivalent affirmation: there is a plan, but good luck, pal. We cannot know it. There are patterns, but a mist of *hebel* obscures our ability to see them. This is why as well, to the consternation of religious moralists, Qoheleth can so heartily endorse a provisional hedonism. "Nothing is better for mortals than eating and drinking, and seeing the soul-benefits of their work. This also, I myself have seen, is from the hand of God" (Eccles. 2:24). The times of laughing and feasting, of synchronicity with the seasons, of stumbling over a hidden jewel of happiness, of catching a good wave amid the undulations of the "times," are gifts from God. While you see a chance — you damned fool! — take it. *Carpe*, emphatically, *diem*. Soon enough, the time will change — tomorrow Lent begins — but tonight, *mon frere*, is Mardi Gras. As they say in Lafayette, *laissez les bon temps rouler*.

The Blueprint in the Book of Job

The book of Job depicts, verse by verse, the avalanche of tragedy that overwhelms a *mensch*, "a serious man," "a righteous man." It seems that there is a conventional set of readings of Job, this ancient account of undeserved misfortune. The book of Job is about protest, they say, or about the inscrutability of the Deity, or about the nature of suffering. Those readings are accurate; the book of Job addresses those ideas and dozens more. Every reader identifies with and understands Job, the Chamber of Commerce, Temple Israel Man of the Year, whose good deeds do not go unpunished. But most readers seem exhausted by the chapters of windy philosophical debate among Job and his friends that dominate the bulk of the ancient scroll and have nodded off by the time the book reaches its narrative climax, when the Creator appears in a whirlwind to explain to Job how reality works. That is a shame, because this text from, probably, the fifth century B.C.E. rivals its contemporary classics from the axial age — works by Aristotle, Plato, and the Buddha — as an enduring statement about what it means to be human. And the book of Job says something very important about the blueprint.

We should recall its plot. A fairy tale opening ("There was a man in the land of Uz") introduces Job, "the greatest man of the East," a kind of Jordanian Abraham. Job functioned for ancient Jewish readers like Confucius does for Occidentals: he is a legendary wise man from someone else's culture. Such a figure is the ideal subject for an extended parable about whether God has lived up to the divine end of the bargain, enforcing the tough love of moral cause and effect. The audience immediately recognizes the sagacity and virtue of the Oriental protagonist, but from a cultural distance sufficiently removed so that the emotional impact of the sage's suffering is blunted. The distancing device of making its hero a foreigner allows readers to approach the book more as case study than as family history.

After Job's patriarchal credentials are detailed, the scene shifts to the heavens where God and the adversary (in Hebrew, the *śaṭan*) engage in a wager. From the standpoint of the history of religion, this Satan had not yet fallen and evolved, or devolved, into the devil, the cosmic Professor Moriarty. Satan in the book of Job is still on the heavenly court's payroll where he serves as attorney general, conducting moral audits and making reports to the Judge of the quick and the dead.

The Lord initiates the review of Job's file by bragging on him. "Have you considered my servant Job?" God asks Satan. "A blameless and upright man." The prosecutor then goes off the deep end, engineering a malevolently ingenious sting operation to see if this tree planted by the waters can be moved from his piety. "Let's turn the heat up and see what Job is made of," Satan, in so many words, suggests. And the Judge, incredibly, grants the motion, allowing Satan to bend the rules of causality to see if Job can be dislodged from his blameless status.

The game has two rounds: first, God allows Satan to destroy all of Job's possessions (including his ten children!); second, God allows Satan to afflict Job with a skin disease. Job maintains his virtuous equanimity after the first trial: "The LORD gave, and the LORD hath taken away; blessed be the name of the LORD" (Job 1:21 KJV). But Job begins to lose it once the final fence that protects his soul, his epidermis, begins to rot away.[12] "In all this, Job did not sin with his lips," the narrator tells us in Job 2:10, but we cannot help but read between the lines and wonder if he has begun to sin in his heart.

This flaying authorized by the Almighty is what impels Job on the odyssey of doubt and debate that is the content of the core of the book of Job, more than thirty chapters of muddy, twisty poetry in which Job engages a trio of hapless friends bent on dispensing their conventional wisdom about how Job must have done something wrong to deserve this chain reaction of calamity. These conversations between Job and his "comforters," Bildad, Eliphaz, Zophar, and, out of nowhere at the end, a new friend

---

12. J. Gerald Janzen astutely noted that Job's skin represents his final "fence" (cf. Job 1:10) (*Job*, Interpretation [Atlanta: John Knox, 1985], 45-46).

named Elihu who jumps on the pile, tell a story, though the plot has been obscured by the poetic format and the uneven condition of the text, one of the most notoriously difficult sections of the Bible. The dialogue at the core of the book is shaped like a legal proceeding, a court case. The underlying metaphor is that Job is filing a lawsuit against God for breach of contract, accusing God of not enforcing moral cause and effect by allowing the righteous to suffer and the wicked to prosper.[13]

Job makes his opening statement in chapter 3. Chapters 4–27 are the transcripts of the testimony and countertestimony of Job and his forensic opponents. (We have not mentioned the courtroom recess of Job 28; more on that later.) In Job 29–31 Job offers his closing argument and pulls off a brilliant courtroom maneuver. Job spouts a crescendo of oaths in chapter 31 (i.e., "If I have walked with falsehood, let me be weighed in a just balance") that in essence function as a subpoena, arousing God to appear in court and answer the charges. According to the ancient logic, you could speak of the devil or God only for so long before eliciting an appearance. God takes the bait, arriving in the intimidating old style, in the whirlwind, riding clouds, speaking thunder, and snorting zephyrs. Job's skepticism has touched a nerve, and God does not speak in a still, small voice in this fable. Introduced, thus, to the contents and flow of the book, we must now slow down and ponder the meaning of the divine speeches in Job 38–41 and what they say about the blueprint.

Chaos Theory

"Where were you when I laid the foundation of the earth?" the Lord thunders in the first of two speeches in response to Job. In that first speech in Job 38–40, God takes Job on a magic carpet ride above the world to show him how exquisitely complicated reality is. Readers often miss two features of the first divine speech, however. The first is that there is a method to the flow of topics in the first divine speech. The Lord does not simply free-associate ("Where were you when I did this? What do you know about ostriches or snowfall or the constellations?"). Virtually every topic that God

13. For the legal argument in the book of Job, see the overview in Samuel E. Balentine, *Job*, Smyth & Helwys Bible Commentary (Macon, Ga.: Smyth and Helwys, 2006). J. J. M. Roberts is credited with first observing the legal metaphor in the dialogues of Job ("Job's Summons to Yahweh: The Exploitation of a Legal Metaphor," *Restoration Quarterly* 16 [1973]: 159-63).

introduces is something that Job and his friends had alluded to in their earlier dialogues. It is as if God had been listening as they spouted their "wisdom," finally had had enough, and now was correcting all their misunderstandings. "Who is this who besmirches [my] design *('eṣa)?*" (Job 38:2). That is the opening salvo of God's self-defense. And though God is addressing Job, this speech could just as well have been aimed at Job's friends. None of them has understood the "design."

In one of his earlier speeches, Job had offered a professorial aside about the constellations.

> "[The Deity] is mighty in strength, . . .
> he made the Lion [i.e., Leo] and Orion,
>   the Family [i.e., Pleiades] and the Chambers of the South."
>
> (Job 9:4, 9)

In the first divine speech, the Lord undermines the credibility of Job's supposed astronomical expertise.

> "Can you bind the chains of the Family [i.e., Pleiades],
>   or loose the cords of Orion?
> Can you lead forth the stars in their time,
>   or can you guide the Lion [i.e., Leo] with its children?"
>
> (Job 38:31-32)

Eliphaz alludes to the rain during one of his orations:

> "He gives rain on the earth
>   and sends waters on the fields."   (Job 5:10 NRSV)

The Lord counters, in so many words, with "What do you know about the rain?"

> "Who has cut a channel for the torrents of rain,
>   and a way for the thunderbolt,
> to make it rain on a land where there are no persons,
>   on the desert that has no humans in it,
> to satisfy the desolate wasteland . . . ?"   (Job 38:25-27)

Imagine the quartet of Job and his friends in the dialogues as peers of the ancient sages who wrote the book of Proverbs. Each takes the stage to offer his observations of the Great Plan, to describe the truths on certain of the blueprint's squares. Then in the divine speeches, the Lord negates their wisdom; not only are they ignorant of the divine perspective in which the small truths connect into patterns, but they do not even know the things they think they know. Eliphaz waxes about the lion (Job 4:10-11); the Lord gets the last word on lions (38:39-40). The mortals cannot get out of their own way, spouting off about onagers (24:4-5), eagles (9:25-26), ostriches (30:29), Sheol (10:20b-22), Leviathan (3:8), and the morning (3:9). The Lord finally has heard enough, and scathingly replies that they know nothing about "his" work, nothing about said onagers (39:5, 6-9), eagles (9:25-26), ostriches (39:13), Sheol (38:17), Leviathan (41:1-34), or the morning (38:12). The mortals debate the "rules," their provincial law of the land. The Lord takes the discussion into realms unlisted in their atlases, to topics ignored in their indices. The human barristers debated in their court what they considered to be "the rules," *the law of the land.* "The law of the land?" the Lord counters with a lesson about deeper, more ancient matters. "Do you mean the law by which the glaciers dropped their boulders on New England?"

In the divine speeches, we learn that Job and his friends have misunderstood the plan. Their proverbs, the contents of the squares of the grid they have filled out, are mistaken. The book of Job had already previewed this, back in Job 28, that poem within a poem, that interlude, that intermission, that court recess, the interpretive center (the *'atnah*) of the entire discourse, that appeared out of nowhere, with no clear attribution, between the end of the dialogues and Job's final speech.

> "Where does wisdom *(hokma)* come from?
>   And where is the place of understanding?
> It is hidden from the eyes of all who are alive,
>   even from the birds of the sky it is concealed.
> Abaddon and Death say,
>   'With our ears we heard a report about it.'
> God understands the road to it,
>   and he knows its place." (Job 28:20-23)

The second important feature about the divine speeches that is often overlooked — though not by the biblical scholar Carol Newsom, from whose commentary on Job I learned it — is that the Lord's survey of creation in Job 38–40 has a distinct Ripley's Believe It or Not quality.[14] God takes Job

---

14. Carol Newsom, "The Book of Job," in *The New Interpreter's Bible,* 4:595-614.

to ocean depths and mountain aeries, to the "land where no one lives / the desert, which is empty of human life" (38:26). God shows Job ostriches, onagers, and ospreys. God makes Job hover over lions on the prowl (38:39-40) and vultures foraging among human corpses on a desolate battlefield (39:26-30). Why does God privilege the predatory and uncanny in this nature documentary? The answer comes in God's second speech to Job. For now, all we can say is that God wants to take Job where the wild things are.

In his second speech, the Lord narrows the view in order to focus on two creatures, Behemoth and Leviathan, the archetypal monsters of land and sea. Here they are: Bigfoot and Nessie, Sasquatch and Moby Dick, the ancient Semitic avatars of every chaos monster in the human imagination. And God claims to have a relationship with them too. "Will [Leviathan] make a covenant with you?" God rhetorically asks Job in 41:4.

In effect, God says, "I have a covenant with chaos. Chaos is part of the plan." Job had not considered that the wild things were part of creation too. In order for reality to function, the Lord instructs Job, there has to be space for the random, chaotic, and wild. This is the deepest magic of the book of Job. It does affirm that God is reliable most of the time, even if that message is overpowered by the tragic notes struck by Job in his speeches. At the end of the book, Job's fortunes are restored and causality is upheld. This is the Newtonian physics that governs the biblical worldview on nearly every other page. This is the Newtonian physics that governs the predictable stop-on-red, go-on-green world we live in most of the time. But in the divine speeches, God takes Job beyond these limits to see the quantum realm where light bends, time curves, the righteous fall, and even chosen people face exile.

After God's second speech, Job replies, "I see," and the spell is broken, the ordeal is over.

"By the hearing of the ear I had heard you,
   but now my eye has seen you.
Therefore I will withdraw [my lawsuit; Heb. *rîb*],
   and I *n-ḥ-m* (resign myself to) concerning dust and ashes
      (the human condition)." (Job 42:5-6)

In Job 42, the final chapter, the poetic tumult resolves to a prosaic happily-ever-after resolution where Job gets back everything he had lost. Some readers find the sunny end of a story that had been so edgy and opaque disappointing. The scholarly beehive is abuzz with theories and speculations about scribal studio bosses who ordered the book's producers to come up with a new final scene, the optimistic extant ending. It could be. Still, the upbeat ending does nothing to blur the bracing and bittersweet clarity that the divine speeches had shed on order and chaos, causality and the random.

Through a series of ordeals, God pushed and pulled on Job until, for a moment and no longer than that, this mortal received a vision of Kugel's "Great Plan," the divine blueprint of reality, and it included space for chaos. Up and down, east and west, to and fro the Lord moved Job until Job caught for an instant a glimpse ("By the hearing of the ear I had heard . . . but now I see") of the divine design in all its beauty and horror. There is a square marked "Chaos." God has a covenant with Leviathan.

The very structure of the book of Job had already demonstrated this; its medium is its message. The book plays with and frustrates the perennial symmetry of all the tripartite structures we long for in discourse. In a world filled with jokes that have three parts and sermons with three points, with Hegelian schemes that have three movements and Marxist eschatologies with three dialectics, with proper stories that contain beginnings, middles, and ends, the book of Job throws a curve. The rhythm of Job is one, two, and . . . the third thing is a little off. In the prologue, Job undergoes two trials (loss of children and possessions; the skin disease), but where is the third? There are two cycles of balanced dialogue with Job and his three friends giving testimony and countertestimony (Job 4–14; 15–21), but then in the third round (Job 22–27) the symmetry breaks down, the speech of the third friend, Zophar, and Job's response to that are missing. There are two big pieces of courtroom testimony, the description of the facts of the case in Job 1–2 and the testimony, pro and con, of Job and his accusers in Job 3–31, and then, just when it is time for judgment and sentencing, a new character, Elihu, breaks the spell and introduces an *amicus curiae* brief that delays matters. In the structure of the book itself, right angles and clearly marked boundaries lose their edges and bend and morph into Dali-esque ellipses. A fascinating character, the Adversary, disappears after chapter 3, and a forgettable one, Elihu, appears in chapter 32. All that is part of the plan too. There are patterns to what we label chaos, there is music to what sounds like noise to us, but these patterns and melodies are hid from the eyes and ears of the living; only God knows their fearful symmetries (Job 28:20-23). Job's complaint is that reality is not on the square and the level; the Lord's response is that the divine geometry is not only Euclidian, it is fractal.

When Job confesses "I see," the game is over and we can return from the wilderness to everyday life in Uz. According to the story, Moses received the Torah, the divine instruction, on Mount Sinai. The book of Job has a climax that is equally epic: on the Jordanian steppes, Job glimpsed the *ʿeṣa*, the divine design.

The book of Job does not say this outright, but we can only conclude that the creaturely freedom that monotheistic religions rightfully celebrate, the dance of choice and risk that makes us human, must extend to all realms, even beyond the human. Tectonic plates are free every century or so to hiccup and produce tsunamis. Every millionth pulse, cells are free to mutate into strange new forms. Meteors, every aeon or so, are free to leave their orbits. Why would God create a world so wild, so free?

Again, the book of Job does not come out and say it, but the only thing I can think of is this: it was all for love. Love cannot be coerced; it can only be chosen. The Creator designed a world with terrifying freedom on the off chance that love might emerge from the chaos. That is the real cosmic wager at the foundation of the book of Job, not the side bet that the Lord and Satan make. And on this matter, the jury is still out.

CHAPTER SEVEN

Conspiracy Theory

The Backstory of Apocalyptic

There are times when chaos gains the upper hand and humans in partnership with God can only hope that God is able, as in the beginning, to subdue chaos.

Around 200 B.C.E. a new type of story emerged in biblical literature: apocalyptic. The word is not Hebrew; it is Greek and it means "revealed." The entire Bible, from one angle, is "revealed," but a fancy word with five syllables, "a-po-ca-lyp-tic," is used to refer to those narratives and poems that begin to emerge in Jewish culture around 200 B.C.E. that are really "revealed." This particular river of revelation branches off from many sources — ancient Syrian and Iraqi myths about battles between Order and Chaos, Persian fables about divine dualities, the increasingly dramatic imagery of Hebrew prophecy — but ever since this new channel of religious discourse began, it has flowed unabated through world culture. Consider this advertisement for apocalyptic that has never appeared in any tract or pamphlet:

Apocalyptic: The Deluxe Package

includes

Heaven and Hell
The End of Time
Armageddon

Angels and Demons
Messiahs and Cosmic Heroes
Hidden Scrolls, Lost Books, Great Codes
Satan

Growing up in late-twentieth-century North America in the Bible Belt, I was exposed to apocalyptic from an early age. I am not a religious scholar who has merely read about this material in books; I have seen the charts. Long before there was big money to be made on Left Behind books around the turn of the third millennium of the common era, there were little piles of money to be made on books about the end of time, such as Hal Lindsey's *The Late, Great Planet Earth,* published in 1970, back in the 1960s and 1970s when overexposure to the Cold War, the Vietnam War, massive social upheavals, and assassinations combined to provide an early wave of premillennial influenza.

I took all this stuff seriously. I was the religious kid in the group. While all the normal kids in high school in the early 1970s were experimenting with drugs, I rebelled from the rebellion by experimenting with God. I read *The Late, Great Planet Earth* with its time charts and hermeneutical jerry-rigging of texts from Daniel and Revelation about Babylon and Jerusalem reinterpreted as referring to Moscow and Washington. And *The Late, Great Planet Earth* was merely the popular version. For the real nuts, like me, there were books sold on tables in the backs of churches holding revivals or gospel music concerts, and available, COD, by mail order through ads in pulpy magazines published in Tulsa and Dallas. This was the real unvarnished truth, lurid, with grainy aerial photographs of Meggidos and Armageddons in Turkmenistan.

A single book in Tanakh, Daniel, contains full-blown apocalyptic literature, and all the genre's potentialities are there. The biblical book of Daniel previews almost all these coming attractions that will be expanded and jazzed up with special effects by later communitarians, sectarians, millennialists, and not a few enterprising evangelical entrepreneurs.

Heaven and Hell

Daniel opens the file on heaven and hell through his allusion to a postmortem judgment. "And many who sleep in the dusty ground will awake: Some to forever life and some to shame and to forever alienation" (Dan. 12:2).

With a few exceptions, the texts of the rest of the Hebrew Bible assume that rewards and punishments are distributed in this life, that God enacts justice in this vale of tears: the righteous prosper, living long enough to see their grandchildren; the unrighteous inherit the whirlwinds of destruction. Though this view was contradicted daily, the ideology held through the First Temple period and began to wither only when generations of deferred Diaspora dreams made it untenable.

In his visions, Daniel does not speak of heaven and hell explicitly. He merely sketches the blueprint of those chambers where the righteous and unrighteous will be housed forever. Other apocalypticists will add the details. Heaven, God's realm above the sky, was already available and eventually became the destination of the righteous. Hell was another matter. This required new construction. Sheol, the Hebrew name for the underworld abode of all the dead, evolved into Gehenna, which was a real place, a garbage dump outside Jerusalem where, legend had it, child sacrifice had once been practiced in the Iron Age. This fiery, sulfurous depression was imagined as the portal to Hades, the place where the unrighteous were imprisoned after death. The morgue of Sheol was remodeled into a torture chamber.

When Daniel wrote about the "forever life" and "forever alienation" that await the righteous and unrighteous, respectively, around 175 B.C.E. in Jerusalem, a Syrian tyrant terrorized the Jewish people. His name, Antiochus Epiphanes, was Greek and he had pretensions to great learning and culture, but he was just another in history's parade of bullies. In the next turn of history, this wannabe would become history, overthrown by Jewish revolutionaries known as the Maccabees, during events that are celebrated each Hanukkah. But before that, there were the bad times that the author of Daniel lived through: life in Diaspora, singing the Lord's song in what seemed like a foreign land. Antiochus Epiphanes outlawed the worship of the Lord, persecuted Jews, and even desecrated the temple by erecting a statue of Zeus inside it and having a pig sacrificed on its altar. And in this crucible of pain, before any revolt was evident, when the bad guys were winning, Daniel dreamed that the martyrs of his day would be rewarded in the world to come. The ancient text in Daniel 12 preserves a delicate leaf of hope in the amber of poetry under immense pressure.

This was a new story. Before Daniel, the Israelite belief was that you went to Sheol, the underworld, after you died. You got your reward in this life. After Daniel, the Jewish and Christian belief was that the righteous lived past death: the Christians talked about heaven, the Jews about 'olam *habba,* the "World to Come." In this text in Daniel, we can see a turning point in the evolution of ideas about what happens when you die. "And the wise ones will glow like the glittering skydome, and the ones who nurture virtue like the stars forever and ever" (Dan. 12:3). This image of the wise glittering like the skydome, of the righteous shining like the stars, this single frame in the slide show of humanity's spiritual yearnings, is our oldest, clearest vision of eternal life. Here in Daniel 12 is one of the first recorded stanzas in a song entitled "The Hopes and Fears of All the Years."

What is the picture here in Daniel of eternal life? It is astral projection, literally. The wise will glitter like the skydome, the righteous like the stars. It is about heaven and going to heaven, but heaven here is not God's celestial city with pearly gates and apostolic border guards and streets of gold. We do not get that stanza of the song until the book of Revelation two hundred years later. Heaven here is the night sky where the righteous live forever as stars. Daniel is saying, dreaming or imagining, that the righteous become stars. And this also has something to do with the righteous becoming angels, because the ancients imagined that the stars were angels and that the angels were stars when they were off duty, when they weren't announcing births to Hannahs or Marys, or protecting George Baileys from despair on Christmas Eves in Bedford Falls.

Remnants of this stage in the history of heaven remain embedded in our culture and are so much a part of the ensemble of our spiritual house that we may not even notice them anymore. When an old cartoon dissolves from the image of a person dying to a new star appearing in the sky, we get it. When we hear children's stories about the littlest angel, we get it. Even when we hear that Latter-day Saints and Swedenborgians imagine that the righteous evolve into angels in the afterlife, we get it, even if we do not buy it. When we are emotionally satisfied to see the hero at the end of Steven Spielberg's film *Close Encounters of the Third Kind* ascend skyward in a spaceship and we feel like this ending completes a story we already know, we get it.

Apocalyptic Elements in Daniel

The final book to be composed that made it into the Jewish Bible, Daniel contains many other elements from the apocalyptic repertoire. In his ecstatic visions, Daniel stands outside of Chronos and can see the markings on its wheel of time. He announces "the end-time" (Dan. 8:17, 19; 11:35, 40;

12:4, 9) and "the last days" (10:14; 12:13). Daniel predicts the eschatological weather: the "wrath that is appointed for the end" (8:19), a "stressful time like has never occurred since nations have existed" (12:1). Times have been appointed, dates have been set (11:27, 29, 35), though they must be translated in vague codes such as "a time, two times, and half a time" (7:25; 12:7) or "seventy weeks" (9:24).

Earthly effects are caused by cosmic battles between angelic princes (10:13, 20-21). A war in heaven rages, initiated by shape-shifting, phylum-bending chaos monsters who emerge from the sea, and will only be resolved when the Ancient of Days intervenes (7:2-22). Angels, for the first time in the Bible, receive names: there is Gabriel the herald (8:16; 9:21) and Michael the cosmic warrior and protector of Israel (10:13, 21; 12:1). All this and more is inscribed in a secret scroll to which the seer is privy (10:21; 12:1, 4). The end of time, ultimate battles, hidden scrolls, angels and demons: they are all there in Daniel.

Satan

The one element of the apocalyptic story that does not appear in Daniel is the devil, though Daniel's four beasts will morph into the book of Revelation's Red Dragon and Beast, both emblems of Satan. "Devil" is the word we use for the personification of evil, for the supreme opponent of God in the almost-eternal battle between order and chaos that takes place in chronological time, and for the archvillain of world literature and culture. A devil-like character begins to appear in Jewish stories outside the canon around the time of Daniel, though the Satan we have come to know and loathe does not explicitly appear in the Jewish Bible, which is the same as the Christian Old Testament.

His names are legion. In the Jewish scrolls attributed to Enoch, a character from Genesis who never died (Gen. 5:24) and so was perennially available to return to visionaries with secret information from heaven, the evil angel was named Semihazah. In the *Apocalypse of Abraham*, his name was Azazel. In Qumran, he was Belial or Beliar; in *Jubilees*, Mastema; in the Gospels, Beelzebul; in early Christian literature, Lucifer. None of this material ever gets sorted out systematically; to this day, all these diabolic epithets remain in play among apocalypticists, fantasists, and occultists. But let us agree here to refer to him by his Hebrew name, "Satan."

"Satan" in the uppercase evolves from a word used about a dozen times in First Temple biblical texts, *śaṭan,* that means "adversary" or "opponent" (Num. 22:22-32; 1 Sam. 29:4; 2 Sam. 19:22; 1 Kings 11:14, 23, 25). In biblical texts from the early Second Temple period, namely, Job 1–2 and Zechariah 3, "the Satan," Hebrew *haśśaṭan,* emerges as the name for an angel who conducts moral audits of humans. What was once a function of God alone — it was God (Elohim) who tested Abraham in Genesis 22:1-19 — becomes the task of a certain angel. In the next era, the late Second Temple period, *haśśaṭan* falls from heaven to become the architect of evil, the father of lies, the ultimate tempter and tester, Satan. The word "devil" is the Greek translation, *diabolos,* of the Hebrew *śaṭan,* "adversary."

At least three stories are told in these extrabiblical texts about how Satan fell. According to "the watchers" myth, Satan was among the angels sent in primeval times to tutor humans in the arts of civilization. These "watchers," as in guardians or babysitters, saw that the "daughters of men" were fair, according to these expansive readings of Genesis 6:1-4; sired giants by them; and were then punished by Michael and his contingent of circumspect angels. Satan is the leader of the remnant of the fallen watcher angels who were spared annihilation, and who subsequently roam the earth bedeviling the humans to whom they remain perversely attracted. As for the giants, the flood killed most of them off, though a few live on in lore as antediluvian relics and monstrous races espied in remote places by ancient and medieval travelers.

According to the "Envy of Adam" myth, Satan did not fall at the time of the flood, but back around day six of creation week, after the Lord God created Adam. In this story, Satan, God's most beautiful angel, refuses to cater to the new member of the family, Adam, created in the divine image. In this account of primordial sibling rivalry, Satan's refusal to kowtow to Adam leads to his banishment. It is no wonder then that he bears such a grudge toward Adam's descendants. In the "Lucifer" myth, the best known of these narratives to moderns because John Milton retold it so memorably in *Paradise Lost,* Satan — the Morning Star, the Day Star, that is, Venus, Hebrew *helel* — led a failed heavenly coup before time and was banished from heaven along with his legion of fallen angels, the demons.

Around the turn of the common era, an epic combination of all these motifs — the devil cannot be separated from the rest of the apocalyptic repertoire — took place that has captured the imagination of audiences ever since and has been remade a thousand times. The apocalyptic epic took its protagonists from the spate of ancient divine combat stories about hero versus monster, shoreline versus sea, and levee versus river — all variations on the theme of order versus chaos. Both Persian and Israelite prophets had already made innovations to this story, merging myth and history, those early attempts in the seventh to fifth century B.C.E. that fused Morning Stars with the King of Babylon, as thus spake Zarathustra, Ezekiel, Isaiah, and Zechariah. These prophets relocated or retemporized the divine combat from cosmic or natural realms to historical ones. The combat does not happen at sunrise or at the eclipse or in the winter or during the drought; it will occur on Tuesday. We might use an idiom such as "the clock is ticking," but for them it was the shadow advancing along the sundial's face. It is there in scenes from Daniel: the beasts are those very tyrants, the kings of Media and Persia and Greece (Dan. 8:20-21). And any day now, any moon now, something is going to happen.

We already had great casting (gods and heroes versus monsters), we already had great scenarios (heavenly battles and underworld journeys) — these features were in the old creation myths — but we needed this element of suspense, the shadow's advance on the sundial's face, to make the apocalyptic story come fully alive. It is the difference between the dramatic tension in Oberammergau's Passion Play and Agatha Christie's *The Mousetrap*. If you know how it is going to come out, if the scenario is seasonal, it is not nearly as exciting as if it is happening in real time once and for all to historical or realistic characters.

In short, the apocalyptic story combines amazing characters (the devil and the demons against God, Christ, and angels), vivid suspense (time is always running out; the end is near), exotic stagecraft and scenery (heaven, hell, Jerusalem, all manner of ancient and contemporary Area 51s, locations that serve as cosmic ports and mythological manholes between realms), and an action-filled plot (a battle or perilous journey). No wonder it has had such a long run on the stage of human storytelling.

The Conspiracy Theory

C. S. Lewis knew a good story when he heard or read one, and his description of the apocalyptic core at the heart of Christianity both captures the qualities that have made it so popular and sketches the conspiracy theory that is its backstory.

> One of the things that surprised me when I first read the New Testament
> seriously was that it talked so much about a Dark Power in the universe

— a mighty evil spirit who was held to be the Power behind death and disease, and sin. The difference [between this view and dualism] is that Christianity thinks this Dark Power was created by God, and was good when it was created, and went wrong. Christianity agrees with Dualism that this universe is at war. But it does not think this is a war between independent powers. It thinks it is a civil war, a rebellion, and that we are living in a part of the universe occupied by the rebel.

Enemy-occupied territory — that is what this world is. Christianity is the story of how the rightful king has landed, you might say landed in disguise, and is calling us all to take part in a great campaign of sabotage. When you go to church you are really listening-in to the secret wireless from our friends.[1]

Lewis wrote this a decade before its publication in the above form, while living in wartime London during the Blitz. The first apocalypticists also knew about living in enemy-occupied territory. A four-headed beast of successive Persian-Hellenistic-Syrian-Roman tyrannies was the evil empire that ruled over their Holy Land. These first conspiracy theorists were oppressed Jewish mystics who claimed to have discovered *the real truth* through documents from the beginning of time that they had unearthed, the testaments of patriarchs from Genesis. They claimed to have heard about it from ancient saints such as Enoch who, since he never died, was free to return and reveal heavenly secrets to mortals. They claimed to have seen it in dreams and ecstatic visions in which angels such as Gabriel visited them. The original members of the Jesus movement were from these precincts of first-century Judahite religion, and the religion that emerged from their movement, Christianity, was suffused with this story.

"In the present age, Beliar is unrestrained in Israel," reads the *Damascus Document* (3.12-18).[2] This devil has authority over a vast empire, "the governance of all wicked people," according to another document of the Qumran communitarians (*Community Rule* 3.20).[3] Under the command of "the prince of the power of the air" (Eph. 2:2) are evil spirits who form

---

1. C. S. Lewis, *Mere Christianity* (1952; reprint, San Francisco: Harper, 2001), 45-46.

2. For the *Damascus Document*, see Michael O. Wise, Martin G. Abegg Jr., and Edward M. Cook, *The Dead Sea Scrolls: A New Translation*, rev. ed. (San Francisco: Harper, 2005), 49-78.

3. For the *Community Rule*, see "Charter of a Jewish Sectarian Association," in *The Dead Sea Scrolls*, 112-36.

an "alliance which results in error and fantasy" (*Testament of Reuben* 3.7).[4] Sinners, consciously or not, "ally themselves with Beliar" (*Testament of Issachar* 6.2) to form an underground criminal organization, a sinister heaven and earth society.[5]

The triad of terror, this mafia of malevolence, is presided over by "Satan and his spirits," a phrase from the *Testament of Dan* (6.1), and is pitted against the angels of light in a perennial *Spy vs. Spy* great game of espionage.[6] Satan is above all the "spirit of error" (speaking of "the Antichrist," 1 John 4:6), "the father of lies" (John 8:44) who disguises himself, according to 2 Corinthians 11:14, as an angel of light, and in the *Testament of Job* as a beggar, the king of Persia, and a bread seller.[7] Things are not as they seem. The truth is out there, and apocalyptic unmasks it, laying bare the wheels-within-wheels machinations behind the powers-that-*seem-to*-be. "For," Saint Paul writes, "our struggle is not against enemies of blood and flesh, but against the rulers, against the authorities, against the cosmic powers of the present darkness, against the spiritual forces of evil in the heavenly places" (Eph. 6:12 NRSV). Our struggle is against Lewis's White Witch of Narnia and Tolkien's Sauron, Sir Arthur Conan Doyle's Professor Moriarty and Sax Rohmer's Fu Manchu. All the portraits of countless fictional criminal masterminds and evil comic book kingpins from Lex Luthor to Doctor Doom are miniatures of Satan. All the world's conspiracy theories, their casts ever changing to fit the social prejudices and fears of their adherents, are mutations of this first apocalyptic story about the devil and his demons.

The Backstory of Apocalyptic

It took immense pressure, of deprivation and persecution among Daniel and his community during the infamous reign of Antiochus Epiphanes, to forge the white-hot images of apocalyptic out of the steely moralistic poetry of Hebrew prophecy. The early chapters of Daniel (Dan. 1–6), for the

4. For the *Testament of Reuben,* see "Testaments of the Twelve Patriarchs," trans. Howard C. Kee, in *The Old Testament Pseudepigrapha* 1 (New York: Doubleday, 1983), 775-828, here 782-85.

5. For the *Testament of Issachar,* see *Old Testament Pseudepigrapha,* 1:802-4.

6. For the *Testament of Dan,* see *Old Testament Pseudepigrapha,* 1:808-10.

7. For the *Testament of Job,* see "The Testament of Job," trans. R. P. Spittler, in *Old Testament Pseudepigrapha,* 1:829-68.

most part, have a completely different texture. These folktales (such as Daniel in the lions' den) address the question of how to sing the Lord's song in a foreign land by offering stories about young people who remain faithful, in various ways, to their Jewish culture, faith, and ethnic identity, and still prosper. The apocalyptic visions in Daniel 7–12 address the question in a different way: rather than sketching daytime coping strategies for living in the Diaspora, they offer nighttime cosmic revelations about heavenly struggles taking place that will result in their vindication.

It is interesting to contrast these two genres and their respective strategies. It is likely that the apocalyptic visions in Daniel stem from a later period than the folktales in Daniel. And we can imagine that the folktales originate in the Persian and early Hellenistic periods when a degree of assimilation and accommodation between Jewish identity and viability and the host culture or occupying power was possible. But in the late Hellenistic period, especially under the reign of Antiochus IV Epiphanes, a Seleucid ruler of Palestine, Jewish culture was suppressed and the temple in Jerusalem was desecrated. Under such circumstances, a different kind of message needed to be heard; in the bleakest of situations, only a supernatural deliverance was imagined.

There is a continuum here that is ambiguous. To some extent faith means "seeing through." Faith means living in two worlds, the real world and the world of justice and righteousness, the kingdom of love. Faith, for Christians, means hallucinating that the face of the poor is the face of Jesus; for Jews, that the face of the poor is Elijah's. Faith means seeing angels unaware in the faces of strangers. Faith means believing in the illogical proposition that self-giving is more powerful than self-aggrandizement and self-preservation. Faith means believing that, despite appearances, the good guys do win, and then living as if it is the truth and not a lie. People of faith straddle the transcendent and mundane. Maybe some folks get it out of balance at times. What is the difference between the eyes of faith and the visions of apocalyptic? I don't know. Is there a difference of intensity or density, a shift in the balance between now and then?

Maybe at times the mundane is so bleak that the only story that keeps faith alive is the cosmic story. It is significant that the most prominent biblical book utilized in the African American songbook is Daniel; Daniel is about living in Diaspora, staying faithful in the day, hoping that one will be delivered from lions' dens, and feverishly, ecstatically hoping in the night for salvation from the principalities and powers of the present.

Most of the backstories in the previous chapters are about the partnership of covenant by which God enlists Israel — and, I pray, many others — to support the fragile network of Providence. Through good works and worship, through vigilant maintenance of the firmaments of justice and peace that restrains the chaotic violence ever ready to erupt, the faithful serve as helpers corresponding to their Creator. But there are times when the chaos is, or seems to be, overwhelming. Apocalyptic was born in such a time. According to its story, the only hope the faithful have during such tribulation is that God, as in the beginning, as in the oldest stories about divine heroes and dragons, can subdue chaos. The backstories have come full circle and the canon ends where it began, with creation. The final platform of hope is the simple and basic truth of creation, that there is something rather than nothing, that we did not will ourselves into being, and that the Creator of the universe chooses Life.

Conspiracy Theory: A Postscript

In the apocalyptic hall of mirrors, where nothing is as it appears, it is tempting to read an even deeper conspiracy behind the conspiracy.

The devil has taken on so many unpleasant chores of the divine administration: testing mortals on Earth, punishing sinners in hell, authoring the repertoire of disasters that thin the herds and forests, injecting periodic doses of chaos that inspire innovation and new growth. Satan is "the opponent," *haśśaṭan*, but his opposition has benefits, forcing God, the angels, and the saints to bring their best game. Satan makes life easier for theists, giving them a focal point for their frustrations, providing them with a common enemy, and freeing worship from the inhibitions of ambivalence. Satan is the personification of the adversity that makes existence possible; in so many ways, Satan is the necessary evil. Did Lucifer volunteer? Was he drafted? Was his primeval heavenly rebellion scripted? Did the Angel of Light empty himself, bedimming his brilliance, in order to do the dirty work that Michael and Gabriel did not have the dramatic range or courage to handle?

It is as if Satan, even after his fall, remains part of the divine government under the deepest, deepest cover. It is as if, on the last day, when all creation gathers in the cosmic temple just prior to the messianic banquet, the Ancient of Days will call Satan to the dais and say, "Even with all the shattered vessels and original sins, love overcame adversity, it was a *felix culpa* after all, and even though it seems familiar, there is something about

Omega that I like better than Alpha. It was worth the journey. Well done, good and faithful servant."

So we must add two more Jewish biblical interpreters to the list of writers to whom this book is indebted, George and Ira Gershwin. It is in their score to *Porgy and Bess*.

Dey tell all you chillun de debble's a villain
But 'taint necessarily so.

CHAPTER EIGHT

Windows

Seven backstories, seven days of creation: all the backstories are about creation, all the backstories are about the dance to the music of time between order and chaos that makes for life. After all the interplay of myth and narrative, of local traditions and creation stories, of tall tales and epic stories, of holy cities and sacred mountains, of Dead Seas and living waters that make up the contents of the Bible, we stand again where we began. The river is widest at its mouth. It was all there in creation.

In closing, let me alert my readers that they may want to back up. I intend to swing for the fences, and try to say something about the theological physics of the Bible.

Western thought is dominated by concern for chaos management. The seven backstories presented here all assume the active voice. Humans are invited (the prevalent Christian view) or drafted (the prevalent Jewish view) to partner with God in chaos management. We are supposed to do something, nay, do a lot of things: perform justice, love our neighbor, follow, hear, seek, endure to the end. Even the apocalyptic backstory has this activist dimension in its canonical examples. It is significant that the apocalypse of the Jewish Bible, Daniel, is an admixture of moralistic folktales and end-time visions. The visionary material, the dream life of faith in the second half of Daniel, cannot be divorced, says the logic of its canonical arrangement, from getting up in the morning and performing the chores of a tenacious commitment to Torah and a courageous refusal to bend the knee before none other than the Most High. The apocalypse of the Christian Bible, Revelation, too admonishes its audience to display "patient endurance," *hypomoné* (Rev. 1:9; 2:2, 19), to remain standing in the face of enormous pressure. Even this most passive of the seven backstories elicits performance. Without revisiting dusty arguments from religious history about Pelagianism (are we saved by performance or saved by grace?), the story of the Bible is not complete without the wisdom of the window stories.

The Window Stories

There are three stories in the Bible about male heroes being rescued from death at windows, and in two of them female characters are their deliverers. We have already seen the first story, the account in Joshua 2 of Rahab saving the Israelite spies in Jericho.

> Then Joshua son of Nun sent two men secretly from Shittim as spies, saying, "Go, view the land, especially Jericho." So they went, and entered the house of a prostitute whose name was Rahab, and spent the night there. . . . The woman took the two men and hid them. . . . She . . . brought them up to the roof and [hid] them with the stalks of flax that she had laid out on the roof. . . . Then she let them down by a rope through the window, for her house was on the outer side of the city wall and she resided within the wall itself. (Josh. 2:1, 4, 6, 15 NRSV)

Then there is the story about how David is saved from assassins sent by Saul when his wife Michal, Saul's daughter, engineers his rescue.

> Saul gave [to David] his daughter Michal as a wife. But when Saul realized that the LORD was with David, and that Saul's daughter Michal loved him, Saul was still more afraid of David. So Saul was David's enemy from that time forward. . . . Saul sent messengers to David's house to keep watch over him and to kill him in the morning. But David's wife Michal told him, "If you do not get yourself to safety tonight, tomorrow you will be killed." So Michal let David down through the window; he fled away and escaped. (1 Sam. 18:27-29; 19:11-12)

These are minor stories in Tanakh, quiet, narrowly focused nocturnal operations overshadowed by adjacent spectacles that take place in broad daylight; in Joshua by the walls of Jericho tumblin' down, and in 1 Samuel by a shepherd boy felling a pituitary giant. But the New Testament writers, so attuned to the dynamics of the Jewish Bible and ever improvising new harmonies on its greatest themes, appreciated the window motif and told their own version of it about the apostle Paul.

> For several days [after Saul's vision on the road from Jerusalem to Damascus] he was with the disciples in Damascus, and immediately he began to proclaim Jesus in the synagogues, saying, "He is the Son of God." . . . Saul became increasingly more powerful and confounded the Jews who lived in Damascus by proving that Jesus was the Messiah. After some time had passed, the Jews plotted to kill him, but their plot became known to Saul. They were watching the gates day and night so that they might kill him; but his disciples took him by night and let him down through an opening in the wall, lowering him in a basket. (Acts 9:19-25 NRSV)

This Christian revision of Tanakh overplays its polemic against Judaism, leading to some flat notes ("the *Jews*"). Still, the basic chords in this story are from Tanakh. This Saul is the new David; the Jewish leaders in Damascus are the new Saul, jealous of an upstart rival's increasing power, bent on assassination in order to maintain power. Paul, nee Saul of Tarsus, reminisces about this event near the end of a letter to the church in Corinth.

Everyone knows about Paul's speech in 1 Corinthians 12 and 13 about how all the esoteric knowledge and mystical prowess — the marks of the spiritual athlete who can prophesy and speak in tongues and perform miracles; the religious version of the hero who slays dragons — do not mean a thing compared to love. For me, though, Paul more soulfully expresses this theme in his speech from 2 Corinthians 11–12 where he is angry and speaking with more emotion and less grandiloquence than in 1 Corinthians 13.

> Since many boast according to human standards, I will also boast. . . . But whatever anyone dares to boast of — I am speaking as a fool — I also dare to boast of that. Are they Hebrews? So am I. Are they Israelites? So am I. Are they descendants of Abraham? So am I. Are they ministers of Christ? I am talking like a madman — I am a better one: with far greater labors, far more imprisonments, with countless floggings, and often near death. Five times I have received from the Jews the forty lashes minus one. Three times I was beaten with rods. Once I received a stoning. Three times I was shipwrecked; for a night and a day I was adrift at sea; on frequent journeys, in danger from rivers, danger from bandits, danger from my own people, danger from Gentiles, danger in the city, danger in the wilderness, danger at sea, danger from false

brothers and sisters; in toil and hardship, through many a sleepless night, hungry and thirsty, often without food, cold and naked. And, besides other things, I am under daily pressure because of my anxiety for all the churches. (2 Cor. 11:18, 21a-28 NRSV)

This is the itinerary of the hero; this is the Christian odyssey. But Paul, following the example of his master who "emptied himself, taking the form of a slave" (Phil. 2:7 NRSV), turns it all around. All this hero stuff, is this the measure of a man?

It is not. Paul continues, "If I must boast, I will boast of the things that show my weakness. The God and Father of the Lord Jesus (blessed be he forever!) knows that I do not lie" (2 Cor. 11:30-31 NRSV). So what is Paul's claim to be the Christian hero? If all the above do not get him into the Hall of Fame, what are the credentials he would present? What is on his résumé? "In Damascus, the governor under King Aretas guarded the city of Damascus in order to seize me, but I was let down in a basket through a window in the wall, and escaped from his hands" (2 Cor. 11:32-33 NRSV).

After all the teeth-gritting exertion and Homeric peregrinations and epic fortitude, in these three stories our big, strong, male action heroes are saved by Rahab, by Michal, by an unnamed cohort of disciples. The heroes are as helpless as babies as they on litters are let down from a window to some kind of safety. The special mark of biblical heroes is not the time when they were strong, but the time when they were weak. Maybe it is just the Baptist in me, but it seems to me that one message of the window stories is that, in the end, we are all saved by grace.

The habits of mind characteristic of cultures shaped by Judaism and Christianity inspire a work ethic and hyper-achievement. They build off the truths of the seven backstories, that God calls humans to actively partner in the struggle against chaos. This emphasis on virtuous good works also, at the same time, breeds the seductive illusion of control. If there is something to the stereotypes of yin and yang, of East and West, of Oriental and Occidental, of orientation toward rising or setting sun, then "Western culture," whatever that means, inspires an essential activism. But in truth, all cultures make busy in and make meaning of the full day. So every truth is somewhere in every culture, even if there are distinct configurations of themes that allow us to employ the generalizations of our various analytic schemes. The window stories remind Jews and Christians that some things are out of our control, that sometimes all we can do is to let go and drop to the ground. These window stories are one of many places where the West opens its orderly, busy house to allow the breezy truth of nonattachment, of letting go, to blow where it listeth.

Saved by grace: that is a theological way to articulate the truth of the window stories. But is there a biological way to articulate it?

Let us recall again the outline of the window stories: a male hero is delivered to life at the threshold of a window, and in two of the three stories, it is a woman (Rahab, Michal) who is the agent of fenestration liberation.

What is the ultimate portal of deliverance? When is the moment when we are most helpless and can do nothing, not a damned thing, but can only allow others to bring us to life? Where is the threshold of life where women stand on one side, to usher us out, and on the other side, to receive us?

There they are in so many biblical stories, the Bible's singing unsung heroes, standing on opposite banks of the birth canal: mothers and midwives. This truth is encoded in the Exodus account of the midwives Shiphrah and Puah (Exod. 1:15-21), whose heroism allows for Moses, Tanakh's premier male action hero, to be born at all. This truth is encoded in the Lord's reply to Job, "Do you know when the mountain goats give birth?" (Job 39:1). The unspoken answer to the Lord's rhetorical question is that the divine Midwife knows; she is there at every delivery. The final chapter to the backstories and the initial and final word of all our stories is that life is a gift. That is the backstory to all the biblical backstories, a simple celebration of the miracle that we were born at all, an emphatic affirmation that "to be" is better than "not to be."

Religion

Religo: that is the Latin verb for "to bind," "to attach," and it is the root of our word "religion." Religion includes more than stories. Religion also includes the enacted stories we know as rituals. Religious stories and rituals serve as binding agents for communal and individual meaning making. Without them, many communities and individuals would fall apart. Religion also provides a means to bind our small stories with the biggest story we can imagine, such as the connection I have drawn between the window stories and the most basic facts of life.

The final story of the Bible might also be told with one word, "God." "God," a derivative of the Anglo-Saxon word for "good," is merely a linguistic accident, a juxtaposition of two very firm consonants around a vowel that binds them together. Utter "God" once and it might seem meaningful; utter it repeatedly and rapidly and you will hear its phonetic hollowness. It is just a word.

It is just one of humanity's thousand words for the Nameless One with Ninety-Nine Names, for the One who is Three and (according to the sacred decametrics of Kabbalah) Ten, for the Un-Imaged who fills our imaginations, for the Unseen we seek to beatifically envision. But the word "God" is also a story in itself. It connotes the ultimate expression of "good." To use it is to tell a story about how creation is *ṭob me'od,* "very *good,*" that all things work together for *good,* that love will win out in the end, that life is not designed to break our hearts, that in the final accounting, as Wendell Berry phrased it, all our "odds be thus made evens."[1]

But is this story of God true? It takes faith to adopt this story even as it adopts us, this binding, adhesive Bible story about how there is meaning because there is Life, and about how we share this story communally as covenanted Israel or as the body of Christ or as the *'umma,* the people, of Islam. But is it true? Whether it has stuck to me or I stick to it, all I can say is, that's my story.

1. Wendell Berry, "A Marriage Song," in *The Selected Poems of Wendell Berry* (Washington, D.C.: Counterpoint, 1998), 150.

Subject Index

Author Index

Scripture References